EXITS AND ENTRANCES

EXITS AND ENTRANCES

GREGORY MCDONALD

HILL & COMPANY, PUBLISHERS • BOSTON

Mcdonald, Gregory, 1937–
  Exits and entrances / Gregory Mcdonald.
    p. cm.
  The first book of Mcdonald's Time^2 quartet.
  ISBN 0-940595-14-1 : $16.95

  I. Title.
PS3563.A278E9 1988   87-32132
813'.54—dc19   CIP

Designed by Milton Glaser, Inc.
Printed in the United States of America

TIME^2

LOVERS AND PANTALOONS

PART ONE: A WHILE AGO...

They decided to go out of the house, so they went for a walk. He had planned to spend the evening in the house with her, but when her father came in and the time came when they knew each other restless, with common, unspoken consent they excused themselves and went out. Her father did not show his disappointment that they would not be there to talk with, but he excused them with the thought that they had a need for movement more than conversation. He pretended he had come into the room and sat down for some other reason, as he felt apart from the youngsters, and he picked up the newspaper he had read and looked at it. They were very polite about their leaving but they could do nothing about the silence in the house after they left it. Her father did not put down the newspaper, for self-respect, but he could not see what he once had read. He listened to the silence until his wife came in. He took her coming as an occasion to put down his newspaper and he asked her if she wanted to sit where he was sitting although she already had directed herself to her favorite chair. He watched her become settled and take up her knitting needles and he wondered that she always had something to do.

"Kids." He folded his hands across his stomach and yawned. "They never tire. You'd think they would welcome a chance to sit down once in a while."

"The Cunninghams might come over for whist, dear. Would you mind?"

"God, I hope they do."

*   *   *

She was down the steps before him. Jumping after her he grabbed her hand, and when they were walking in step he swung their arms in a wide, playful arc. Crossing the lawn the grass flicked against their shoes in the silence. The hedges put them out of sight of the house. The sound their shoes made on the sidewalk matched their heartbeats and, to their breathing, gave a quarter-beat.

"It always smells good after a rain."

"Mnn."

"What did you say?"

"Mnn. M as in *Mnn*, n as in *Mnn*, n as in *Mnn*."

"Conversational old bear. George, look at the moon, the crowded sky, the moonlight making little patches here and there among the trees. . . . Just look at those stars! I want to reach up and grab down a handful of them. Don't you want to reach up and grab down a handful of them?"

"Mnn."

"Nothing affects an old bear. George, breathe that air! Golly, the air after an electric storm. Don't you love the air after an electric storm? And don't say 'Mnn.'"

"Why can't I say 'Mnn'? Can't I say 'Mnn' even once? You're mean not to let me say 'Mnn.' You don't love me, not to let me say—"

"Yes, I do, George Brice."

"Then I may say 'Mnn'?"

"Yes."

"All right, I think the stars above your head are beautiful, and the little patches of moonlight on your hair are beautiful, and I love the air you breathe after an electric storm."

"The air really is good."

"Because you breathe it."

"You're sweet."

"Mnn."

"Oh, George. Daddy should hear you now, 'sighing like a furnace.'"

"I'd rather be a bear than a sweet anything."

"'With a woeful ballad made to his mistress' eyebrow.'"

"What does your father say about me?"

"What?"

"I want to know what your father thinks of me."

"Why?"

"Tell me, Marty. I want to know. I want to know what your father says about me."

"He says you're a nice gent."

"I really want to know."

"That's what he says: 'That George Brice is a nice gent.' That's all."

"He doesn't say 'nice gent.' No one ever said 'nice gent.' "

"Ask him."

"He thinks I'm not good enough for you."

"Oh, George."

"And he's right, too, Marty. I'm not good enough for you. I'll never be a judge or anything. I'll never even be a lawyer. I think he knows this is the only suit I own; maybe the only suit I ever will own."

"Daddy doesn't pay attention to things like that. Not Daddy. He likes you."

"I've arrived in this suit every time. How could he help but notice? I hate this suit."

"I think it's rather nice."

"You don't suppose he was hurt, do you?"

"When?"

"When we just left. He looked sort of hurt."

"Nonsense. When you've got as many things on the mind as Daddy has, those things don't mean anything. Heavens, Daddy's too important to get hurt or upset over things like that."

"I don't know. I thought he looked sort of hurt."

"No."

"I was noticing the other day the other pants to this suit are getting pretty shiny."

"Really?"

"The Judge never had a pair of shiny pants, I'll bet."

"Are you serious? You don't know Daddy if you think a thing like that. Are you being serious?"

"I'll bet the only shiny trousers he's ever seen in his life are worn by the criminals who appear before him in court. If I appeared at your house in my other pair of pants he'd probably sentence me to thirty days or thirty dollars."

"You don't know Daddy at all. You think he was born sixty and sophisticated?"

"I guess I do. Black diapers and a judge's mallet instead of a rattle."

"You are funny."

"I can just see him banging the mallet and shouting 'Order in the nursery!' "

"I've got to tell Daddy that. I simply must."

"No, Marty, don't."

"Why not?"

"Please don't, that's all."

"You're afraid of Daddy! You are, too; don't say you're not. Why, George Brice! I never suspected you of it! Big, broad-shouldered you! Poor little Daddy!"

"It's just that I feel foolish when—"

"No need to feel foolish. You don't know Daddy. Few do. It's not that we're ashamed or anything, but, well, in this America of ours, not everybody's background is what you might think. Sometimes it's best to leave things to people's imaginations."

"What do you mean? He's a judge of the District Court—"

"And his father died when he was a little boy leaving his mother destitute. She had to take in laundry, and he had to help her. How do you like them apples?"

"Sure. And he saved the life of a rich man on a runaway horse who staked him to law school out of gratitude. You can buy that story anywhere for a dime."

"You can't buy Daddy's story for a dime. Not the story of Daddy and his mother and of my mother and her father."

"How much have I got in my pocket? Let's see. Twenty-four cents. No. Twenty-seven. How am I doin'?"

"Not for any price. Daddy's father was a stevedore on the docks of New York. An immigrant. A piano shipped from Europe fell on him and killed him. He was an hourly worker, so he didn't leave even a full week's pay."

"Marty, is this the truth?"

"The absolute truth, so help me God. Surprised?"

"Your grandfather—. Your father—"

"Just listen. So his mother started taking in laundry. What else could she do? Take in laundry or starve to death. But they lived in the slums, and people in the slums do their own laundry. Somebody had to walk miles a day collecting and delivering the laundry, and that job fell to Daddy. He left school. Daddy never had a formal education beyond fifth grade. His mother taught him how to read and he read everything he could get his hands on. *Shiny pants:* just envision my Daddy, as a little kid, walking through the streets of New York City carrying a laundry basket in both hands. On top of the laundry there'd be the book he was reading as he walked. Every few feet he'd have to put down the laundry basket to turn the page."

"He needed me to invent an automatic page turner for him."

"Maybe that's what you would have done, George: invented something. My father just slogged along reading, bumping into things. He never could have known where he was going. Funny, when you envision it. My grandmother saw how he would read, and pushed him on, got library books for him. When he was old enough, he got a job driving a bread wagon early in the mornings. Days he worked in a grocery store. Nights he spent in the library. He says all those years driving the bread wagon he kept a copy of *The Republic* in his pocket. He loved *The Republic*. He still does."

"I never read *The Republic*."

"I only read it because of Daddy. And at school."

"I never went to school. And I never read *The Republic*."

"You went to school, George. In Columbia Falls."

"High school."

"That's more formal education than Daddy every had. Not many people go beyond high school. The only reason I did was because Daddy wanted me to so much. You don't know another girl in town, or in Columbia Falls either, I expect, who has gone beyond high school. And, frankly, it makes me feel like a freak. You'd think I have consumption or something the way everyone avoids me. Sometimes I wish Daddy hadn't wanted me to go to Cambridge so. Oh, well."

"I'm glad you did."

"Why?"

"So your father could send you. I think he probably enjoyed it. I think he probably needed to send you to school. Too bad he never had a son."

"So they say. But Daddy believes in strong women, women with their eyes open. He has every reason to."

"Because of his mother?"

"She wasn't educated, of course, not above the reading and writing level, but he says she earned his law degree as much as he did. From the age of fourteen on, he supported her totally. She stayed home, went to the libraries, organized his work for him, got him the right books, at the right time, kept him on track. He'd be driving the bread wagon or pushing the broom around the grocery store while reading, studying, thinking. At night he and his mother would sit at the kitchen table and go over everything again and again. They discovered the law together. She would ask him the questions and he would answer. Neither knew anything but what they had from the books, but they would argue and reason together. That went on for years.

"Finally one night after years of this, he came home and after supper he got the books out. He sat at the table and waited for his mother to sit down, but she never did. She kept puttering around, doing this and that. Finally he spoke to her.

" 'No, Daniel. Not tonight.'

"After all these years they had sat down together every night he could not understand her not sitting down that night.

" 'Don't you feel well?'

" 'Nervous, Daniel.'

" 'About what?'

" 'About your taking the Bar Examination tomorrow.'

" 'I'm taking the Bar Examination tomorrow?'

" 'The time has come to find out if we've been wasting our time. If we have, we should stop, and fill our heads with something else. One way or the other, you've got to get out of your mother's kitchen.'

" 'I can just walk in and take the Bar Examination without ever having been to school, and no one says I can't?'

" 'Those are the rules as I read them. We'll see. We'll see how this country works, or doesn't.'

"My father says he just stared at his mother puttering around the sink. I guess he's the sort of man who studied for the sake of studying. He says he had never given the examination a thought. As long as he had been reading and learning it had never entered his mind that he might be wasting his time, or that he had a goal.

" 'Why on earth haven't you told me?'

" 'Daniel, if you had known about the Bar Examination, you might have wanted to rush things, for my sake. Or you might have gotten nervous as the date approached—as I have. We've been doing just fine. Now you're as ready and as relaxed as you're ever going to be. Tomorrow will prove all.'

"My father had never taken a real examination in his life, not even a test since the fifth grade. Of course he didn't sleep that night. He went into the examination frightened stiff.

"He came back to their little apartment at suppertime. He went over to where his mother was sitting by the window. He knelt down beside her.

" 'I failed.'

" 'You can't know that yet.'

" 'I do know it. I read the first question and the whole room, the whole world, went blank on me. I don't remember a thing I wrote. I might have written poetry, for all I know.'

" 'Daniel . . . ' My grandmother took my father's head in her hands. She said, 'Succeed or fail, Daniel, what you wrote, to me, is poetry.'

"My father says no one has ever said anything better to him: *Succeed or fail, Daniel, what you wrote, to me, is poetry.* Without her being a lawyer, or having any education at all, to speak of, my grandmother taught my father the law, educated him.

"He not only passed, he got the highest marks that year, all without ever having gone to school. To me, what happened between those two people, my father and his mother, is the poetry."

"So. Okay. Your Daddy knows about shiny pants."

"He says if his mother had never been able to say another word to him, for some reason, he would have been satisfied at her saying that, that about the poetry."

"It was a lovely thing to say. Where is she now, your grandmother?"

"She died a long time ago. I never knew her. She must have been quite a person. Quite a person. I don't think a day goes by my father doesn't mention her.

"Then my father was a long time coming up in the world. He didn't have any money to open an office, of course, so he continued at his jobs, driving the bread wagon and sweeping up the grocery. He had the highest mark on the Bar Examination, but the big firms were not interested in a nineteen-year-old boy who did not know how to tie a necktie. He would know better what to do now, of course, but then he had absolutely no connections. People around the neighborhood who knew he had become a lawyer came to him when they were in trouble, and, he says, only because he didn't know better, and they couldn't afford better, he'd go to court with them. He would win some of the cases, but, still, no one could pay him. He felt it was enough to have worked for, just to help his neighbors when they needed help.

"Once there was a young girl in the neighborhood indicted for murder. She had confessed to the police and had proven a detailed knowledge of the crime, so the police were satisfied with her guilt. The neighborhood people asked my father to appear in court with her. He changed her plea to not guilty. She screamed and swore at my father to such an extent right there in the court the judge had her removed. My father then proved that the girl's brother was the murderer. The newspapers gave that case some attention.

"The next week my father received a letter from a law firm out here, a partner in a law firm, named Barton, offering to pay my father's way out here to visit the firm to discuss employment. My father saw it as a chance to get himself and his mother out of the city, so he came along.

"On my father's first night out here, he was invited to Barton's new home. My father said he had never seen a place so elegant. It's still a mansion in his eyes, but, honestly, George, it's just a nice house, not all that much better than ours.

" 'This is my daughter, Mister Foster.'

" 'How do you do, Mister Foster? It's so nice to meet you. My father has told me how well you did with that case in New York. Here, sit next to me. Why would a girl sacrifice herself for her brother on a murder charge?'

" 'Love,' my father croaked. He had never seen such a house, such a woman as Miss Barton.

"My father loves to say that the very first word he said to Miss Barton, my mother, was *love*.

"Barton said, 'My daughter hopes to walk you through the local stores tomorrow, Foster. In a town like this, the clients like you to dress in local fashion.'

"Graceful, uh? You worry about your shiny trousers, George. Grandfather Barton had to get my mother to buy clothes for Daddy and show him how to wear them before he could even be walked in to meet the rest of the firm."

"I'll never say another word about shiny pants. Maybe I should have worn them to the house."

"But, you know, my father's mother never did move out here with him. He did well in the firm, made good money, bought this house, married Miss Barton, my mother, supported his mother, of course, went back to see her often, but she refused to move out here. She said he had to make his own life, his own American life; he'd do better, his family would do better without his old immigrant mother around. He never agreed with her on this, or accepted her feeling this way, but he couldn't argue with her successfully. She was one strong lady, I guess. She came to visit only twice. On her first visit, after looking around, she said, 'Daniel, you've made me so happy. I'll live to see you a judge. You'll see.'

"My father had never thought of being a judge. It was a whole new idea to him. So, as they say, he put himself in the way of an appointment, to make her happy.

"She came out to visit once again. She sat in the courtroom the first day he sat on the bench. Then she went back to her old neighborhood in New York. A month later my father heard she was dead."

"Well."

"Well, what?"

"Well, I guess I won't say *Mnn*."

"My mother calls him a *good man*. I like that idea. I like the idea of having a father who is a *good man*. Of course, his being a good man sometimes makes me feel less than good."

"Now what are you talking about?"

"Sometimes he says things that make me angry and I forget that he drove a bread wagon and my mother had to teach him how to buy a real shirt and a real suit and real shoes, and then I get twice as mad at myself."

"Sure you get angry at your father. Only natural. You don't get *really* angry, do you?"

"Very."

"What?"

"Very."

"About what, for Pete's sake? How could you get *really* angry at a father who's done all he's done?"

"Oh, George, I don't know. He's taken to hanging about, oozing ... what? ... self-concern. Like just now, when we were in the living room and he came in. You're right. He didn't really have anything to say to us, but I guess he really didn't want us to leave, either. Sometimes I come across him all alone, and he's just sitting there, looking tired and scratching the hair behind his ear. He seems to enjoy making jokes about how old he is. He doesn't get up out of a chair, or climb the stairs without saying, 'Oh, I'm getting old, Marty.' That makes me angry."

"Not really. Come on, Marty. It doesn't make you really angry."

"It does. The other day I came across him out in the yard and he was just standing there all by himself. I asked him what he was doing. Do you know what he said? He said he was just wondering where he'd like to be buried! Just think of it. He was standing all by himself in the garden wondering where he'd like to be buried. Ghoulish."

"What did you say to him?"

"When he said he was wondering where he'd like to be buried? I said, 'How about under that rose bush?'"

"You didn't."

"That's where we buried Sausage, our old dog."

"Did he mind?"

"He laughed."

"But did he mind ... ?"

"I was wondering if he is sick, maybe, if he quietly isn't feeling well. Maybe he knows there's something wrong with him but he's just not telling anyone, but he himself can't help thinking about it, you know?

"So, I asked Mother about it the other day. She said she's been worried, too. She told me she'd gone down to Doctor Godfrey to see if he knew if there was anything wrong. Doctor Godfrey said he thinks it's just Daddy's age. He said many people become depressed at sixty-five, think they haven't much more to look forward to. Sometimes, he said, some people just sit down for the rest of their lives, as if they were afraid to spend time on anything, because they feel that life moves faster if they are doing something, anything. That's why I almost screamed today when Daddy mentioned retiring."

"He did?"

"Yes, at lunch. Like a little boy, he was already sitting at table. He didn't get up when we entered. He's always stood up when we entered, especially mother. He acted pretty glum all the time the waitress was serving us. It was swordfish, his favorite, but he ate in silence as if he weren't tasting his food. My mother and I exchanged glances all during lunch. We didn't know what was coming.

"Finally he said, without even looking up from his plate, 'What would you think if this swaybacked old horse put himself out to pasture?'

" 'Don't you feel well, Daniel? If you go to bed, should I call Doctor Godfrey? Where don't you feel well?'

" 'I am not talking about retiring for the afternoon. I am talking about retiring for life.'

" 'Daddy—'

" 'Well, what's the matter with that? Other men retire. Can't I retire? Is retiring something only other men can do?'

" 'Retiring isn't *doing*, Daniel. It's *not* doing.'

" 'That's the idea.'

" 'But Daniel, you never said anything.'

" 'About what, retiring? When is one supposed to mention it, on the wedding night? For God's sake—'

" 'Daniel, please. If Martha doesn't mind your language, I do. Now what's this about retiring?'

" 'Well, what do you think of it?'

" 'Think of what?'

" 'Now, Helen, don't give me that vacant look. You know damned well what I'm talking about.'

" 'You're thinking of retiring.'

" 'Yes, damn it, I'm thinking of retiring.'

" 'Is there an especially hard case on the docket, Daniel?'

" 'After all these years on the bench, I'll never see another hard case. Just a bunch of damned fools acting selfishly and getting caught because they're stupid—that's my considered opinion of jurisprudence after umpteen years on the bench. How long must one suffer fools?'

" 'Correct me if I'm wrong, Daniel, but it is my belief you worked hard to become a lawyer, then a justice of the District Court—'

" 'I worked hard, yes, but under the direction of my mother, then under the direction of your father, your direction. I had no personal ambitions, other than to survive. America is such a nation at this time in history that a fellow who does a reasonably good job of surviving is given success and responsibility beyond his personal dreams and then just kept at it, without his ever having lived, until he is planted in the soil to enrich unconceived generations. Where am I in all this?'

" 'Don't get excited, Daddy. No one's angry.'

" 'Who's excited? I knew this would happen the minute I brought it up. You both look like soulful puppies at me, and I'm supposed to apologize for ever having brought it up!'

" 'No one's saying anything about apologizing, Daniel. It's just that we fail to understand. You mean you are thinking of retiring from the bench and going back into practice. Well, I think it might be something to think—'

" 'I'm talking about *retiring*, period. Retiring like a driver of a bread wagon retires, like a bread wagon horse retires, like a grocer retires. I'm almost seventy—'

" 'You're sixty-five, Daddy. And not a bit swaybacked.'

" 'And a mighty lively sixty-five, too, I might add.'

" 'See, everybody's fighting me. Making jokes. At least in a courtroom you have an impartial judge or jury or something. Damned few lawyers can argue their own case in front of their wife and daughter, that I know.' He put his head on his hands and looked gloomily at his plate. 'Everybody's dying.'

" 'Everybody's not dying.'

" 'Well, there are damned few who aren't! Will Bartlett over in Lincoln. Tom Jewells. Harry Belknap. Harry! He's just a kid. He used to work around the office before he even graduated. I used to call him "son." Oh, God. One night, in the snow.'

" 'That was last winter, Daniel.'

" 'That makes it better? That time is passing? Time is passing, damn it!'

" 'That's no reason to get excited now. Are you sure you feel all right?'

" 'Of course I feel all right! I've always felt all right! Harry always felt all right! I feel well enough to die!'

" 'Daniel, you're being silly. If you have something wrong with you, tell us and we can do something about it. Otherwise, I just don't understand this. You love your work. I don't know what you'd do without it.'

" 'I wouldn't do anything. I'd retire. I'd go out to the pasture with Pigeon and Penelope and chew grass.'

" 'No, now Daddy. Seriously. What would you do?'

" 'Well, I'd buy a boat and we could take trips.'

" 'You've never been on a boat.'

" 'Well, I'd grow radishes. All my life I've liked radishes, but there have never been any on the table. Maybe if I grew my own, I'd get to have some.'

" 'Daniel, in all our married life, never once have you mentioned a particular fondness for radishes.'

" 'You see? Where am I in all this?'

" 'You're just tired, Daniel. It's warm for September. Why don't you slip upstairs for a little nap before you go back to the courthouse? You don't have to go back right away, do you?'

" 'I knew it would happen! God almighty, I knew it would happen. Try to discuss retiring, just once, after all these years, with my wife and daughter, and they try to put me to bed for a nap!'

"I've never seen him so upset. I thought he would break something. Daddy's always been so calm. I just don't understand, not at all. It's not like him, not a bit like him."

"Did he say anything else?"

"Oh, yes. He got his hat and came back into the dining room and yelled at us, 'Don't be surprised if they bring me home in a Black Maria with a shroud over me!' and slammed out of the house back to the courthouse."

"That was today?"

"Yes. Today. It's serious, George. What if he did retire?"

"What of it? I gather your family won't starve."

"Well, what could he do? He'd just sit around and grow old. He'd take up reading the newspaper as a full-time occupation and before you know it he'll be writing letters to the editor!"

"Boy, think of wanting to retire with all he's got. I sure wouldn't.

I'd love to have just one day walking around town with everybody calling me 'Judge' and 'Your Honor' and asking me my opinion on everything."

"Can you imagine him retired?"

"No. But it is his life."

"Grow radishes! He went out and worked with the gardener one afternoon a year ago, and the gardener had to work on Sunday to straighten everything out."

"Maybe he's just tired."

"He's not tired. He's depressed about something."

"Let him have some radishes."

"George, do you think Daddy needs a fancy lady?"

" 'A fancy lady!' Marty—"

"Oh, I don't mean *need* one, George. But maybe he would *like* one. That's what I mean. Do you think he could *use* one, George?"

"Marty, he's sixty-five years old."

"Oh, Agnes says some men are never too old. Some men."

"I think your father has a bit too much dignity to be climbing down from the bench so he can climb some back stairs into a perfume fog."

"He might want one, all the same."

"No, Marty, it's not that. It's probably as Doctor Godfrey says. He just wants to slow down, so the rest of his life won't seem so fast."

"Will you feel that way?"

"Life isn't going fast enough for me, right now. There are things I want—"

"I'm sure you wouldn't go around the house saying macabre things. You'd never feel sorry for yourself. I can't see anyone wanting to take up feeling sorry for himself as a full-time occupation. It may be all right Sunday mornings, but—"

"How can we understand, at our age, what it feels like to be sixty-five? Will you think me terrible if I tell you something?"

"Why would I?"

"Because I'm ashamed of it."

"Then I'll be ashamed of it, too. What is it?"

"I'm ashamed of myself."

"I'll never be ashamed of you, George."

"Wait until you hear this. Talk of ghoulish. The other morning I was down in the Square. It was early, the stores were closed, the streets were empty, not a soul around anywhere. It was very, very quiet. Around the corner, slowly, slowly came a hearse. It was followed by carriage after carriage. The horses' hooves were muffled.

The carriage frames didn't even squeak. They crept around the corner at me, as if *to* me. The men driving the hearse, all the people in the carriages were sitting up straight, facing forward, dressed in black, white-faced, grim-mouthed, clearly not speaking to each other. I was all alone in the Square in the bright early morning, and this horrible black cortege appeared from around a corner and began creeping at me."

"So? An early funeral—"

"I began to laugh."

"George!"

"I couldn't help myself. It struck me funny."

"Did anyone see you?"

"Of course they saw me. I was roaring with laughter, as if someone had just told me the funniest story in the world. The drivers of the hearse gave me a look that was so sour it made me laugh even harder."

"What did you do?"

"I tried to pretend I was crying. I put my hands over my face. Finally, doubled over with laughter, I turned my back on the cortege. Then I realized I was bowing backwards toward them, waving my fanny at them, and *that* made me laugh harder. I couldn't stop."

"George, that is shameful. What did you do?"

"Nothing I could do. I couldn't stop laughing. The whole thing was so ghoulish, and so *at* me, this long black thing creeping across a bright morning ... "

"Did it make you feel nervous? Was that it, George?"

"I don't even have that excuse. It made me feel happy. Young. Strong. Brave."

"Nothing wrong with that."

"There's something wrong at laughing at a funeral, Marty."

"It's not very nice, of course, but I suppose it is wonderful to be able to laugh at passing funerals. You've never seen Daddy as a funeral passes: stricken, somber, pale, averting his look as if to avert death itself. You were more aware of the brightness of the early morning than he would have been. Hey, George. Consider this moment: the stars, the moonlight, something electric in the night; we feel happy, young, strong, brave. We don't avert life."

"No."

"Do you feel it, George?"

"Yes."

"I feel it in my veins. I feel light, as if I have no body, the way a poet must feel, so light I could exist on a peak, drink the air and eat the fog."

"I feel that way, with you."

"Do you, George? I believe you do."

"I do, Marty."

"You had to laugh at the funeral. It wasn't nice, but don't be ashamed. It was absurd that people should use such a beautiful morning to dress in black and think of death."

"Do we feel this way because we have each other?"

"Because we have each other. Because we are young and know it."

"Here. Stand still, Marty. Stand perfectly still. Listen."

"What is there?"

"Just listen. Be quiet and listen."

"Yes."

"Do you hear it?"

"Yes."

"What do you hear?"

"Listen."

"No, I want you to tell me, Marty. What is it you hear? Tell me, Marty."

"I hear the music."

"What is the music?"

"The breeze in the cooper beech. And the silence around it."

"And what is it you feel?"

"I feel the breeze against my cheek. In the tree the breeze is only a sound in silence, but, against my cheek, it is cool. I look up to see the breeze and do not see it. I see the stars, which have come close together tonight, as if to look. The stars' silence above the breeze is expectant."

"Waiting for us."

"To see what we will do. What will we do, George?"

"Look to the stars."

"This is a strange moment. It is dark, but with moonlight. We are together, but alone. Why should I be afraid?"

"Are you?"

"Your arm around me makes me braver."

"My arm around you makes me brave."

"Brave to do what?"

"To kiss you?"

"Will we be one then?"

"No. But we will be more together."

"Oh. George. Oh."

"We make the stars happy, Marty. They expect a lot from us."

"As long as you don't make me expectant, too, George."

"You make me happy, Marty."

"Oh. Oh."

"Here, let's sit down."

"Where?"

"Here. On the grass."

"This is old man MacGregor's lawn. He'll kill us if he sees us."

"He won't see us. His lights are out. He's probably in bed. We won't hurt his lawn."

"The grass is cool. Don't you love to touch grass, George? It's so cool and brisk."

"*Mnn*."

"George, when can we be married?"

"Oh, it will be a long while yet."

"Why? Why can't we be married this weekend? No, that wouldn't be proper."

"No, indeed it wouldn't."

"But we want to be married soon."

"What we want is not always what we get."

"Don't you want to be married soon?"

"Of course I do. I want to be married tonight. But we can't. I don't see that we can be married for a long time yet."

"Why? Why can't we be married, George?"

"Because I'm poor."

"Oh, George."

"I haven't a thing."

"You have. You've got everything. Daddy didn't have anything."

"He had this house before he married your mother."

"That was different."

"That was no different. Anyway, you have to finish school."

"Not really. I don't really have to finish school."

"Don't you like school? You always said you liked school."

"I do, George, but it isn't necessary. I mean, no one, especially a woman, needs to go to school. Heavens, what could I do when I get through? Teach? I don't want to teach. Haven't the patience."

"You'll want to teach our children, won't you?"

"Yes, certainly. That's different. I won't be able to teach them *King Lear* anyway."

"Why not?"

"Time they're ready for that, they won't respect me. Anyway, I will have forgotten."

"Well, someone had better know what they're talking about when they start babbling *Lear*. I won't. They ought to have respect for one of us that way."

"Sounds like we're planning to have monsters."

"We just might. Never can tell."

"George, I want to be married. Now. You want me, don't you, George?"

"Very much."

"How much?"

"Very much."

"Kiss me, Mister Brice."

"Can do."

"Why, Mister Brice! Wherever did you get so much kissing practice?"

"You."

"Just me?"

"No one else."

"You never kissed another girl?"

"Never."

"George . . . "

"Never in all my life. There was a girl. We were thirteen. On the next farm. One day . . . "

"One day?"

"Just one day. That's all. But I've never kissed a woman before. Never."

"Was she nice?"

"Fat."

"How fat?"

"Some days you couldn't tell her from the barn, when the fog was runnin'."

"That isn't nice. You going to go around talking about me like that?"

"You going to get fat?"

"How do I know?"

"You don't look like a barn."

"Not even a bit?"

"Not even in the fog."

"What do I look like?"

"Um. Let me see. What does Marty Foster look like? I think you look like a Morgan filly early on a spring morning, cavorting around, being frisky and playful. I think you look like a sailboat pirouetting in the wind."

"A horse and a boat."

"What do you want me to say? You're beautiful, you're ravishing, you're like a woman on a magazine cover? You're not. I wouldn't want you to be like that."

"Okay. For you I'll be a boat. Not sure about a horse. All right, I'll be a horse for you, too, if you kiss me again."

"There."

"Don't say *there* like that. Like Daddy paying the ice man: *there*."

"What do you want me to say?"

"Something romantic. Exciting. Something Cyrano de Bergerac would have said."

"Don't know the gentleman. With a two-dollar name like that, though, I doubt I could spell what he might say."

"Whopee. Try whopee, George."

" 'Whopee'? Not Whoopee, or whee—"

"No. Whopee. Try it."

"Whopee. Whopeewhopeewhopee."

"That's better."

"Phew."

"What will our children be like?"

"Oh, they'll all have black eyes. One apiece. And they'll all have teeth missing. Front ones. I had all my teeth missing at one time."

"How many?"

"Teeth? Oh, about six."

"I mean children."

"Oh, about six."

"All right. Six in print dresses with shiny faces and pigtails. And they'll each have a favorite doll named Baked Bean."

"Did you have a doll named Baked Bean?"

"Yes."

"Boys don't have pigtails, this part of the world."

"Girls shouldn't have black eyes—not too often, anyway. Not as a regular thing."

"I'm not sure we're talkin' about the same kids, Marty."

"We'll have to have twelve, then. Six of each. I wonder what they'll really be like. I mean, will they really love us?"

"If not, I'll beat 'em."

"I love them already. I love them, and they don't even exist. How can that be?"

"We've got the jump on them. Guess we'll have to remember that. Already we're ahead of them in love."

"Does that mean I'll always love them more than they love me?"

"We've got a head start."

"That's sort of sad."

"Not now."

"What?"

"It's not sad now. Maybe one day it will be, but not now. They'll love us. Why wouldn't they? What are we doing? Sitting here on the grass in the dark wondering if our kids love us as much as we love them and we don't have any kids; we're not even married yet."

"It is sort of silly, isn't it? Maybe my love for them when they don't even exist is really my love for you. Do you think a woman's love for her children might really be her love for her husband?"

"I do think a woman's love for her husband helps her to love her children."

"I think maybe one has to love specifically in order to love generally. Do you know what I mean?"

"No."

"You have to love someone, to love everyone, anyone."

"Only by loving one person can you love the world?"

"Yes. And if you love no one, you can't love everyone, the world.... Poor Mister MacGregor. All alone in that dark house."

"He's a mean old man. Throws sticks at kids and stones at dogs, what I hear."

"Do you think he sleeps in a double bed? I would feel very sorry for him if he sleeps alone in a double bed."

"Maybe he doesn't sleep."

"Look at that little, dark old house."

"I wonder what makes him so mean."

"He never married."

"Do you suppose he never, ever had a moment like this, a summer's night, moonlight, a slight breeze, sitting on a lawn, loving Marty?"

"Not being loved all your life must be terrible, awful. What could he think about?"

"He must distract himself, find other things to think about, something to fill the void."

"What else is there? A person, people ... "

"Heaven, hell, life."

"Do you think he ever *wanted* to be alone?"

"Maybe he just never wanted enough *not* to be alone."

"George, I've never been alone. Never really wanted to be, besides a few minutes now and then, of course, to sort out my heart and mind."

"Perhaps if you've always been alone . . . "

"George, I don't want to be alone. Don't ever let me be alone."

"We'll have each other, Marty, in sickness and in health, through fat times and lean. . . . You know what I'm going to say when the minister asks me to respond to the marital vows?"

"I do? I don't? What?"

"I'll say, '*Whopee!*' "

"You would, too. Anything to put Mother under the pew."

"Your Mother doesn't seem depressed at all."

"No. She wouldn't be, when Daddy is."

"Women. Cry at weddings and cheer everybody up at funerals. You going to be that way?"

"She keeps telling me I don't love them enough."

"Marty . . . "

"Do I act indifferent, George? She says I act indifferent; I never listen. I don't need to listen. When you live all your life with people, you know what they're going to say before they open their mouths. She thinks I'm selfish. She never says so, but I know she does."

"How could your mother think you're indifferent and selfish? I mean, really?"

"I don't know. She just does. This last Christmas I wanted to go out to Katie Doyle's in Newton. She has a brother, and he goes to Yale, and I was sick of the Harvard types, and . . . I didn't know you then. Katie has a nice family, a big house, and . . . her brother's sort of cute. I had only seen him through a window. I thought it would be fun. I wrote my parents in November asking them if it would be all right. '*Certainly*,' they wrote back—both of them. '*Certainly. Go ahead. Have a nice time.*' Two weeks before Christmas, I wrote to them again, to make sure they didn't mind. '*Of course we don't mind*,' they wrote back. '*Have fun!*' So I went."

"You were about to tell me about her brother, weren't you?"

"Oh, George. He blew his nose like a horse, just like a horse. He took snuff! I never saw anybody take snuff before. Lord knows where he got it. Katie didn't know. He'd stuff it up his nose, sneeze, play with his handkerchief, then blow his nose exactly like a horse! Awful!"

"Glad I'm not cute . . . through a window."

"Well, anyway, when I came home this spring I knew there was something wrong. Something just told me so. I could tell the minute I walked in. I thought there had been something in the letters, too, come to think about it. The letters had been sort of reserved, I thought. They didn't sound like Mommy and Daddy. I knew something was wrong.

"Well, the night after I got home I was up in Mommy's room, waiting to go down with her. She was at her mirror fixing her hair, and when Marie went out she asked me why I hadn't come home for Christmas. I didn't know what to say.

"I said, 'Well, I wrote you why. I wanted to go out to Katie Doyle's in Newton. Her folks are awful nice, and they invited me so sincerely. Anyway, it would save the long trip home.'

" 'Do you think that was enough reason?'

" 'Well, yes. They really pressed me to come. I had spent several Sundays with them. It would have been impolite to refuse them.'

" 'What about your parents? Oh, never mind me, Martha. The house was a little empty without you, dear. I'm only trying to say we missed you. Do forgive me.'

" 'Shouldn't I have gone? You wrote me—'

" 'It is perfectly all right, dear. Your father was a little disappointed, though. If it weren't for that, I never would have brought it up.'

"I felt badly. I didn't see why, if they wanted me to come home, they didn't write and tell me.

"The very next night, after dinner, I was out on the lawn with Daddy, and he said, apropos of nothing, 'Martha,' he said; 'it wasn't quite Christmas around here without you. We went over to the Wrights' Christmas Day. Embarrassing, having to say you preferred to spend your Christmas somewhere else.'

" 'Daddy!'

" 'It's all right, pet. You had every right, and I'm glad you did what you wanted to do. I think your mother was a little upset, though. Try and speak to her about it, will you, pet?"

"I felt terrible, George. I felt as though I'd slapped my parents in the face! How could I know they'd feel hurt, or embarrassed? I wrote them twice!"

"You didn't know."

"I certainly didn't."

"They may have felt you didn't want to come home."

"It wasn't that at all. I had just never been anywhere else for

Christmas. Every year since I was a little girl we've gone over to the Wrights' for Christmas day. First year, I smashed my finger in the door."

" 'Smashed'?"

"Well, banged. It got squeezed."

"Which one?"

"That one. You can see a little scar even now."

"Not in the moonlight."

"Of course not in the moonlight, silly."

"I'll hold it, and the scar will go away."

"I don't think wanting to do something different for Christmas makes me 'indifferent' and selfish, do you?"

"Not as long as what's-her-name's brother blew his nose like a horse."

"I hate the thought I hurt my parents."

"They missed you. That's nice."

"You think so?"

"Mnn."

"I missed them, too. I must tell them I missed them. Maybe they don't know."

"They love you. You love them."

"That is nice, isn't it?"

"Very nice."

"I swear I don't know why these things have to happen: everyone getting upset over nothing; we love each other just the same. Useless anger . . . George, we'll never get angry at each other, will we?"

"Of course we will."

"Oh, no. Say we won't. I won't marry you unless you say we won't. I'm not going to have a husband I can be angry with."

"All right, then. We won't. We won't ever be angry with each other."

"Never? Say never."

"Never."

"Good."

"I didn't think it was worth fighting about."

"George . . . "

"You'd only get angry . . . "

"George, my love for you is like, is like a . . . "

"A what?"

"A kitten. All soft, and warm, and purry."

"Kittens scratch."

"Will you scratch me, George?"

"Where does it itch?"

"Oh, George."

"Oh, Marty, what I'll do for you ... "

"What will you do for me?"

"Everything."

"Tell me what you'll do for me."

"I'll build a world for you, and everyone in that world will honor you."

"Tell me reality, George. I love to dream."

"I will become rich and build you a palace and fill it with satins and fine glassware and china; all the wood will be marble, and all the metal will be gold. And there will be a servant for your every wish."

"Doesn't sound like much of a place for kids."

"I'll do better than anyone, because I have your love."

"Does love mean that much?"

"What else does man have to work for but his woman?"

"Don't say 'woman,' George. It sounds so animalistic."

"Woman. Man."

"We shouldn't be out so long. My parents will worry."

"That's all right. I'll offer to marry you."

"Fresh."

"Telling them we're going to get married ... will your parents like the idea of our getting married, Marty?"

"Why wouldn't they?"

"They couldn't do without you over Christmas. How are they going to feel when someone comes along and tells them he's taking their daughter away from them for the rest of their lives?"

"They expect that, sooner or later. It's natural."

"All they know about me is that I'm poor, uneducated, own one suit—"

"If my father didn't like you, he wouldn't have come into the living room tonight. Come on. We should start back."

"He did come in, didn't he?"

"Will you get up and come?"

"Your mother didn't come in."

"She was out in the kitchen telling Cook what to buy tomorrow in the shops. She does that every night after dinner. She likes you very much. She told me to ask you to dinner."

"You didn't tell me."

"Some night next week. Thursday, maybe. Daddy always likes fish on Fridays. Now will you come?"

"Just brushing off my trousers."

"Will you take my arm, Mister Brice?"

"May I buy you a ring, Marty?"

"A ring?"

"An engagement ring. Later, a wedding ring?"

"Sure."

"That's it? 'Sure'?"

"Sure."

"I mean, I know we've done a lot of talking. I've never been sure."

"Since I met you, George, I haven't been able to picture life without you."

"I wake up at night, and feel you in the bed beside me, and reach out for you. I miss you when I haven't had you. Marty, will you marry me?"

"Sure."

"Does that mean, yes?"

"Yeah."

"Say 'Yes,' damn it!"

" 'Yes, damn it!' "

"Whopee."

"Anything to get you walking me home."

"Whopee whopee."

"I shouldn't tell you this."

"Tell me."

"You'll laugh."

"Maybe."

"I'm learning to cook."

"Whopee whopee whopee whopee whopee!"

"You're laughing!"

"What would people say if we ran down the sidewalk in the dark holding hands? I feel like running."

"They'd probably say we had burglarized old man MacGregor's."

"They'd say, 'There goes exuberant youth!' "

"They'd say, 'There go a couple of lunatics!' George, don't pull me! These darn skirts! I'll fall."

"Shucks."

" 'Shucks.' You're crazy."

"I'm in love, and I'm happy!"

"This is a good moment. A great moment."

"Marty, what I am going to do for you, for our kids, for us!"

"I asked you to take my arm, not swing it off."

"I remember once I was out in the barn and I had built a machine. I had spent all afternoon on it, and it was beautiful. It had been raining. All morning I had been rubbing the leather, and we had finished cleaning the stalls. It was a good rain, a welcome rain. It was spring and the potatoes were in and the ground was smelling so sweetly. You'll never know what spring is until you smell the ground in Columbia Falls in the spring. All winter there is snow all through Maine, and the ground is very unfriendly. You can break a plow if you start plowing too early in the year because there are clumps of ice in the ground. But the spring does come, and the ice melts below the ground and the juice from the pine needles sinks into it, and it is beautiful to smell it then.

"In the morning while I had been working I had been smelling the smell and feeling the spring in my veins. And I had thought of a contraption I could make, and I remembered the places I could find the things I needed. I thought about it, and I became happy while I thought for I knew it would be beautiful. There was an exuberance in the air, and my work began to go faster as I thought. The contraption just grew in my head. I planned every inch of it and saw just how it would be.

"I ate the noon stew and pudding quickly, and went out to the shed and began to work. I went up to the loft and dragged down all sorts of things. I got out the hammers and saws and I built and built until the thing began to take shape before my eyes. I never stopped to look at it, but worked and worked. Finally, when I was almost through with it, Eddy came into the shed.

" 'What's the matter, George, aren't you hungry?'

"He looked at the machine in wonder.

" 'Is it suppertime already?' I never would have thought it. 'Didn't we have lunch just a few minutes ago?'

" 'Few hours ago, and more. What on God's greenin' earth would that be?'

" 'Oh, it's—it's a—well, Eddy, take a guess at what it is.'

" 'Is it for digging potatoes out of the ground?'

" 'No, it doesn't do that.'

" 'Well, then there would be no guessing.'

"I set the thing in motion. There was a belt that went around two wheels. One wheel was counterbalanced by weights to keep it moving, and the other wheel was notched so that every time it went part-way around, a ball would fall out onto a ramp. The ball would roll down the ramp and plop into a bucket of water. It was a very beautiful contraption.

"Ed watched the contraption work, the first wheel, the second wheel, the ball rolling down the ramp, then plopping into the water. He watched the operation several times without saying a word.

" 'What does it do, George?'

" 'Do? The wheels go around, the ball falls out of its notch, rolls down the ramp, and goes into the water.'

" 'Why?'

"The machine ran out of balls. The contraption stopped. There was silence.

" 'George,' Eddy said. 'If a machine doesn't do work, then you can't say it works.'

"I was crushed. I looked again at my silent machine in the barn. I saw it differently.

"It was totally useless.

"Then I found myself hungry. I went in to supper.

"I had thought it wonderful I had made wheels go around, balls roll, water splash. I hadn't assigned any purpose to it.

"Everything has to have a purpose, Marty. Just working isn't enough. Before I met you, I was just working. Now I've got a reason to work."

"That's beautiful."

"See how I need you, Marty? I expect I'll always have to work. But there's no accomplishment without a goal."

"I'm your goal?"

"Making a life for you, for us. I'm not a doctor or a lawyer, but I have hands that work and an eye that can see things before they exist, design, invent things. Maybe someday, because I just won't be working uselessly but I'll be working for you, for us, I'll create something the whole world will want, and then you'll have your palace where all the wood is marble and all the metal is gold."

"A servant for every wish?"

"What can say no to us? I can work. I've worked in the fields and in the woods in the rain and the snow. I can create things. In the machine shop where I work now, at Winslow's, I can take a simple machine apart, take things out of it, add things on to it, and come up with a different machine altogether, a machine that does altogether different work."

"That's wonderful, George, but listen, all that really isn't necessary. As long as I have you—"

"Listen. I haven't told you. The other morning Mister Winslow called me into his office and asked me to sit down. That's pretty good, you know, to have Mister Winslow himself, the owner, invite a machinist, a kid from northern Maine, into his office and ask him to sit down.

" 'George, what's this about that blacksmith shop offering you a job?'

" 'Yes, Mister Winslow.'

" 'Well, what about it?'

" 'The Northern-Pacific Railroad.'

" 'Blacksmiths.'

" 'Well, they wanted me to go to work for them.'

" 'Are you going to?'

" 'No, sir. I told them I'm happy working here.'

" 'Glad you said that, son. May sound funny to hear me say it, George, but trains aren't going anywhere.'

" 'Sir?'

" 'They're nothing but a bunch of blacksmiths over there. That's all they'll ever be, to their dying day.'

" 'Yes, sir.'

" 'You work for railroads from here on in, all you've got is a maintenance job. Isn't that right?'

" 'That's what I thought, sir.'

" 'You'll never get a chance to take part in building something new, of your own.'

"I didn't know what he was talking about, Marty, so I didn't say anything.

" 'You made a good choice, George.'

" 'Thank you, sir. Mister Winslow.'

" 'I'm going to build myself an automobile, George, a Winslow car, and you're going to help.'

"Marty, I jumped in my seat.

"Grinning, he put his hand on a thick folder on his desk. 'Got some of the plans right here. Even got some start-up financing. From a bank in Chicago, George. Banks around here seem to feel the future of the automobile is limited to a few daredevils who won't mind ending up mud-splattered and rattled to death.'

" 'A car!'

" 'That's right, George. To hell with calling it a horseless carriage. Strip right to the only three letters that make any sense. C-a-r. Car. The Winslow car. I'm betting on the gasoline kind, the internal combustion engine. If you want to work with steam, go work for the railroad, maintain their teapots on wheels. Electric cars will just plug along. Internal combustion, George. You know what internal combustion is?'

" 'No, sir.'

" 'Stick with me, and you will. You're one of the best machinists we've got, George. You're young and you're bright and you're good with your hands. George, we're going to build the damndest automobile this world will ever see.'

" 'Yes, sir!'

" 'That's fine, George. I sort of thought you might be taken by the idea. I'm happy to tell you about it, but I'd be pleased if news of this didn't get talked about in the machine shop just yet.'

" 'I understand.'

" 'Some of our labor force isn't as open to new ideas as you are, George. Doubtlessly some of them will head straight for the railroad. George, did I tell you we had a son?'

" 'They say so down on the floor.'

" 'You're damned tootin' we did. The biggest eight-pound boy you ever saw. We named him Theodore after Mister Roosevelt. There's a man I've always deeply admired.'

" 'Yes, sir.'

" 'Well, you come up to the house and see the boy sometime. Mrs Winslow will be pleased to have you.'

" 'Yes, sir. Tell me: when do we get started?'

" 'On the Winslow car? Just have to cross a few more t's and dot a few more i's. You be thinkin' about it, George. I'll be glad to have you thinkin' about it. Meanwhile, I'd appreciate it if you didn't announce our plans to the other machinists just yet. The world will know about the Winslow car soon enough.'

"A car, Marty! An automobile! I'm going to start building automobiles!"

"The internal combustion engine, George."

"That's right."

"Sounds dangerous."

"Why?"

"Internal combustion. It means something that blows up inside itself."

"I guess it does."

"Supposing it blows up outside itself?"

"We're going to make automobiles! And Mister Winslow took the trouble to bring me aside and tell me himself. He's a wonderful man,

Martha. He'll make wonderful automobiles. And I think he'll give me a chance to show him what I can do. I think maybe ... "

"You're talking so fast, George."

"I think maybe someday I can give you a big house, and the kids will be all right, going to school, riding ponies ... I can see them."

"I can see them, too, George."

"Do you think if I told your father about all this, he'd see? He'd see that if I don't have anything else, at least I have a chance? A chance to make a life for us, to make you happy?"

'I'll be happy, George. He'll see that."

"It's not much of a start, but it's something. Marty, I can't wait for the future."

"We've been gone a long time."

"Don't go in just yet."

"Why don't you come in, George? We could tell them now. I expect they're just playing whist with the Cunninghams."

"No. After I get the ring. I have to have something to show them. Otherwise it's just talk."

"Come in. I don't want to break off a moment like this."

"A moment like this doesn't belong in the house. Penny for your thoughts."

"I'm thinking how wonderful you are. How whole."

"Whopee. You're the one who makes me whole, Marty."

"Whopee."

"Thanks for making me whole."

"We have to let them know I'm back. I suppose I have to go in."

"I suppose."

"Mommy and Daddy will be wondering where I've been."

"We've been for a walk to the stars and back."

"I'll tell them that."

"To the future and back."

"Once more, George. Just once more."

"Whopee. Is that better?"

"Much better."

"How much better?"

"Very much better."

"I don't think your Seranus fellow would have said *Whopee*."

"Cyrano. Maybe not."

"Cyrano. I think he would have said *there*."

"Maybe. Try it."

"There."

"That's you, George."

"Is that all right?"

"That's fine."

"Am I all right?"

"You're wonderful."

"There."

"I have to go in. They'll hear us."

"Let them."

"They never expected me to be gone so long. It's dark."

"It was dark when we started."

"I hope they don't see the grass stains on my skirt."

"Shh. They'll hear."

"You're the one—"

"I know, I know. But it's that sort of night."

"I really must go in. Don't hold me."

"You're holding me."

"It's that sort of night."

"There."

"I like the way you stand at the bottom of the steps. You make a nice figure. You look like a lover."

"I am. I am a lover."

"Good night, lover."

"Good night, Marty."

After finishing up in the kitchen, she came to the door of the den. "Oh, you've lit the fire."

"Yes, I thought I'd sit up for a while."

The den looked homey to her. There were the new reddish-brown drapes she had made last year and she was glad to see how they suited the scheme of the den. The firelight played nicely on the drapes, the red and yellow American oriental carpet, the red leather sofa and chairs.

She noticed that even in the firelight his hair was white. She only noticed that sometimes, now, usually when they were alone. She couldn't remember their hair turning white. There hadn't been a moment when suddenly it was white, or a day when it seemed more white than the day before.

Now their hair was white, in every light.

"Are you going up right away?" he asked.

"I thought I'd take a bath and maybe read."

"Go ahead."

She came into the room and sat beside him on the sofa. She did not want to leave him staring into the fire all by himself. "What's the matter, Pop?"

"Nothing. Not one thing. Never been happier in my life. For the first time, I'm free."

"Good for you."

"For the first time in my whole damned life, I'm free. Come 'ere."

"What do you want, Mister Brice?"

"I want my wife. I want to put my arm around my wife, feel her close beside me, and I want her to help me look into the fire. You are still my lover, aren't you?"

"Surprised?"

"Yes. You've stayed young, while I've gotten old."

"You haven't gotten old."

"Oh, you don't think so!"

"Well, not any older than I am anyway. And I'm vivacious—"

"And very pretty."

"And you're handsome—"

"And very old. How long have we been married, Martha? God, it's more than forty years. It's forty-one years last June. What a hell of a thing."

"What is?"

"What a hell of a thing to realize. I've spent forty-one years with the same woman, and I've enjoyed it. Never thought I could have."

"We've been good friends."

"Too good. Something abnormal about that. I wonder what's wrong with us."

"We're nice, and we've made an effort—"

"And we've had some good luck—"

"And some failures. We must admit those. No couple ever spent forty years together without failures."

"You know, in this firelight your forehead is just as smooth . . . I have the same urge to kiss it I had forty years ago."

"Watch yourself, Mister Brice. I'm a married woman, you know."

"Do you think your husband would mind?"

"No. He wants what's best for me."

"Whoopie. Do you remember that? Whoopie?"

"No, it was *whopee.*"

"That's right. Whopee."

"The night you asked me to marry you, George: you were so determined. You insisted I say nothing but *yes.* "

"I've told that story enough times. When I asked my wife to marry me, she said, 'Yes, damn it!' "

"I never did."

"Well, I think you did."

"I'd already said yes enough times before you asked me. Really, I couldn't understand your insisting upon a simple answer."

"Do you feel any different now?"

"What do you mean?"

"I mean about the whole thing. You know."

"No. I don't feel a bit different."

"I don't."

"Neither do I, Pop. I mean it. It was wonderful then, and it's wonderful now."

"That's good."

"Yes, that's pretty good. It's pretty good when you can say that after all these years."

"Well, we're pretty good people."

"Especially you and me."

"And me and you."

"You're being silly."

"Congratulations, Mother. If I had a drink, I'd drink a toast to you. I'd say, *Congratulations, Mother.*"

"You were always pretty good at giving toasts."

"I mean it. Congratulations."

"Thank you, dear. And congratulations to you, too."

"At giving toasts, I'd beat you on the five-mile track any day."

"You know, it's been some time since I've seen you, George."

"Where have I been?"

"I'm not sure. George moved out about the time that fellow Pop moved in."

"The last time I saw George was in the waiting room of the maternity ward. I think he died of acute nervousness."

"Poor man. Then what happened?"

"This fellow Pop took his place. Much more mature than George, sedate, cool and collected. Much more responsible. Much more realistic. Much more worried. He's the guy who took you and Paul home."

"Poor Pop."

"He wasn't a poor Pop. He was a good Pop."

"Having to be so responsible."

"He enjoyed the challenge."

"Sometimes he was so responsible he almost drove me crazy."

"How do you mean?"

"He babied me. He babied me and mothered the baby. Almost drove me crazy."

"I did not."

"Oh, yes, George. You were worse than all young fathers put together."

"I don't believe it."

"You were. Sometimes you'd insist on feeding the baby when the baby didn't need or want food. Then you'd come asking me what was wrong with the baby. You'd change diapers when they didn't need changing. Then I'd find all the diapers in the soiled bucket."

"No. Say it isn't so."

"It's so, George. You never knew the difference between a dry, fed baby and a wet, hungry one."

"I changed wet diapers. I remember. Truth is, you were insulted by my help."

"You'd do things to the baby just because you had time at that moment, or happened to be passing by, whether the baby needed it or not."

"I was useless?"

"You were cute."

"I was not cute!"

"You were, you know. Then you used to laugh at Paul when he was doing the same foolish things as a young father. Margot told me about Paul's foolishness as a young father, and I told her about yours, and we laughed and laughed together about it."

"You mean, you spread feathers in the wind about me?"

"Feathers?"

"Yes. From the top of the hill."

"Oh, like the woman."

"You're the original. Go gather up thy feathers, woman."

"They're your feathers. It's not my fault if the wind took them."

"You brought them up the hill."

"I just fluffed them around a little."

"It would be quite a job, picking up all those feathers."

"Isn't that the point of the story? Anyway, Margot was the only one I told. I doubt the feathers spread around very much. Margot needs to laugh at you."

"What do you mean, Margot needs to laugh at me? No one needs to laugh at me."

"She does. Poor dear is scared to death of you."

"Don't be silly."

"I really think she is. You must be nicer to her."

"I am nice to her. But just because my son fell in love with her doesn't mean I have to love her too, does it?"

"Pop, no one is asking you to love Margot. You just treat her too nicely, is all."

"You just said I don't treat her nicely enough."

"I mean real nice. You always talk to her as if you'd just met. 'How do you do, Margot. So nice to see you again.' She's your daughter-in-law! How many years have Paul and Margot been married?"

"Why don't you stop calling me Pop?"

"I've always called you Pop."

"Not always."

"I can't help it. You became Pop. I called you Pop for the sake of the kids, so they'd know what to call you. You call me Mother. Or Martha."

"Makes me feel like a grandfather."

"You are a grandfather."

"Yes, but I'm George, too. As long as I have you, I'm George. When I don't have you, I'll be Grandpop. 'Go get a lollipop from good old Grandpop.' 'Go wipe the drool off Grandpop's face.' I can anticipate that a while longer."

"What's making you act this way?"

"Nothing. Call me George."

"Why did you stop calling me Marty?"

"You don't know?"

"Was it because I grew up, too?"

"How could you know? I guess I always thought you just understood."

"What's so funny?"

"Big event in my life. Funny now, but I was dead serious then."

"When?"

"You remember that place we spent our honeymoon?"

"Of course. Nicest place you could have picked."

"Once I had my car, I went all over the state for a year before we were married, just to find the exactly right honeymoon place for us."

"I never knew that."

"You were finishing up school."

"The Jorgan Quality Inn."

"That's right. That's where my vanity got deflated for once and all."

"Pop, you were never vain. George."

"I was that day. Arriving at the Jorgan Quality Inn. With my beautiful new bride, my Marty. After that wonderful wedding your parents gave us. Wearing my beautiful new suit, under my duster. As much as anything, even as vain as I felt about my beautiful new bride, I was proud to be driving my new Winslow car, a car I had helped to shape and build. It was shining like a mirror. Spoked wheels. I thought I was the cat's meow."

"You were, George."

"I drove up the drive to the Jorgan Quality Inn with all the stateliness the Winslow could muster. I remember it backfired only once, and that was all right, because it got the people on the veranda watching us arrive. Remember the elm trees that lined each side of the driveway?"

"Yes. They were wonderful."

"Tall ceilings, crystal chandeliers, wide, cool verandas."

"It was a family hotel, long gone now."

"It was just before dinner and there were a lot of people on the veranda, women talking, men playing chess, reading newspapers, kids sitting on the steps. People were playing croquet on the lawn across from the driveway. I drove in and pulled up right in front of the main door.

"I helped you out your side of the car. Then I was showing the bellman how to unstrap our luggage.

"Suddenly I heard the kids on the steps giggling. A few men were chuckling. A woman's voice sang out, 'Marty! Here, Marty! Stop that!'

"I looked, and there was this dog, this horrible, foolish looking dog, clipped and curled, all pompadoured up, with a plaid ribbon tied in a bow around the topknot on its head, peeing on one of the spoked wheels, peeing on my car!"

"I don't remember this at all."

"My eyes sought out the woman who had yelled at the dog. I shouted, 'What did you call that dog?'

" 'Marty! Stop that this instant! Come here, you naughty dog!'

"I yelled at the woman. 'Stop calling that dog Marty!'

" 'But her name *is* Marty!'

" 'Well,' I stammered stupidly, red as a valentine, pointing to this foolish-looking crittur that was still peeing on my Winslow car, 'That's not a Marty dog!'

"The bellman dropped a suitcase on my toe. Standing one-legged in the driveway like a stork, sore foot in hand, instead of yelling what I wanted to yell, in front of all those kids I yelled, 'Marty!'

"That got everybody roaring with laughter. They really appreciated that."

"I don't remember that at all. I just remember what a nice time we had. Everybody was very nice to us."

"Sure they were. We were the comedy act of the week."

"Funny what we don't know about each other."

"Destroyed by a dog. A peeing dog."

"And that's why you stopped calling me Marty?"

"For the longest time, every time I said Marty I couldn't see anything but that foolish-looking dog peeing on my Winslow."

"It bothered me, that you stopped calling me Marty."

"It did?"

"Of course. The first year we were married. Before Paul was born. I worried about it. That was a hard time, for me."

"It was?"

"Yes. Those were the worst days, I think."

"Why?"

"Oh, for the first few weeks we were married it was all right. All day long I'd be happy waiting for you. I'd arrange flowers, which you'd never notice. After a month or two, the same old you would come in the door at night, saying the same old things, *Wonderful day. I'm hungry. How you been?* You wanted food, sex, sleep, all in quick order. Things had changed, deeply changed. You didn't call me Marty anymore. Suddenly I was Martha. I didn't know your life had been changed by a foolish-looking dog peeing on your car."

"The dog was called Marty."

"I hadn't even noticed we had crossed paths with a dog called Marty. You had never mentioned being upset by it."

"You were there."

"So? So a dog was called Marty. All I knew was that during the first weeks of our married life you began calling me by my more formal name."

"Sorry."

"I rather envied you, that first year. You'd go off to work in the morning truly excited about what you were doing."

"We were making about the best car produced in America at that time, for the best price. Every day someone would think of something new for it, some improvement. Wonderful days."

"You had something else to do. There are only so many times a day you can make a bed, clean the kitchen, dust the parlor. There are only so many ways you can arrange daisies."

"Were you unhappy?"

"No, no. I've never been unhappy. I just never knew why you didn't call me Marty anymore."

"The silliest things ... I'm sorry. I didn't know."

"Of course you didn't. You and I have been talking to each other for almost half a century and there are still things we haven't said to each other, questions we didn't ask, things we haven't told each other."

"Married nearly half a century, and we still have things to learn about each other."

"In justice, we should begin again. Nice to meet you, Mister Brice."

"Nice meeting you, Mrs Brice."

"We've been down the wooded path together, but we have had to see away from each other."

"There have been bears in those woods."

"I suppose there have. There have been. No couple can ever become a world of two, except in a fairy tale, 'And they lived happily ever after.' No disturbances."

"To stay together, a couple has to fight off the world, sometimes with their backs to each other."

"I'm very happy right now. Aren't you?"

"Very happy."

"I'm comfortable."

"I don't feel sixty-five."

"That's saying something."

"I don't feel sixty-five but everyone says I'm sixty-five. Every morning I have to get up and shave that sixty-five-year-old guy in the mirror. That way, women are luckier than men. Women don't have to look at themselves in the morning, if they don't want to."

"How old do you feel?"

"Right now?"

"Right now."

"Right now, sitting here with the fire sparkin' away in front of us, with us doin' a little sparkin' of our own, mind, I feel about twenty-five. If you asked me to get up and shift that log, I might feel about forty-five. Pretty young for a man to be put on the shelf."

"You haven't been put on the shelf."

"Now we are where I always knew we would be. If we were lucky. Alone. Marty and George. Alone together. And on the shelf."

"We aren't on any shelf."

"What would you call it?"

"Retired."

"Put on the shelf. I wasn't even asked to agree to retire. The expectation seems to be that when you turn sixty-five you have this mad compulsion to go fishing. I don't have a mad compulsion to go fishing. I get enough fishing on the weekends, in season."

"You don't have to go fishing. You can give in to other mad compulsions. You can do whatever you want."

"Sure. We'll do whatever we want. We haven't talked much about this. What do we want?"

"Oh, to visit the grandchildren, bake cookies for the Girl Scouts, and ... "

"Great. I've worked all my life so you can bake cookies for the Girl Scouts, free of charge."

"I like the Girl Scouts."

"Okay. But what are we going to do?"

"Well, you can get in more golf, more fishing up at the camp—"

"Don't say 'fishing.' Fishing, at least the way I do it, is a break from life. It isn't life. Neither is golf. What's my life now?"

"Well, why don't you putter? You're an inventor, Pop. Start a project. Invent something."

"The automobile's already been invented."

"There are lots of things that haven't been thought of yet."

"Like what?"

"I haven't thought of them yet. But you can."

"All they invent these days is formulas. Equations. Mathematical wriggles that are supposed to prove something. The automobile is the only machine I've ever cared about anyway."

"You can work on something."

"Do you know how many better can openers America has to her name now? Do you know how many can openers you have in your kitchen? I was out there the other night—"

"When?"

"The other morning. I couldn't sleep. It was about three o'clock. I came down to count the can openers."

"You went down to the kitchen expressly to count the can openers?"

"Yes. I began wondering how many people had invented better can openers. How many can openers do you think you have?"

"I have no idea."

"You don't collect them, do you? I mean, you don't have the hobby behind my back of collecting better can openers?"

"No. Not one of my mad compulsions. How many do I have?"

"You have nine different can openers. And I expect you're fairly average. Think how many there must be! All these fools have invented better can openers. Worse, they've struggled to get them manufactured. And, somehow, they've all gotten the message across to you that you cannot live without this particular better can opener!"

"I seldom use can openers. Tuna fish. Mushroom soup."

"I found some things in your kitchen I didn't even recognize. There's a thing with three legs and a disk, and one big claw. Looks like someone sent from Personnel."

"That's a potato peeler."

"A potato peeler, see? And another thing that looks like the grill of a car, with a big, ugly nose on it—"

"That's for carrots."

"You need a machine to peel a carrot?"

"It dices them."

" 'Invent something,' she says. I don't even like diced carrots."

"You eat them all the time."

"I do?"

"You love them in salads."

"Mother, I cannot now direct my attention toward inventing something that does something to something I've never even noticed!"

"George, why are you getting mad, in the middle of a nice evening by the fire, at a carrot dicer?"

"I'm not getting mad at a carrot dicer. I'm just mad at the whole thing."

"What whole thing? Life? You can't be mad at life, Pop."

"I don't like being benched involuntarily when I played a good game. It isn't fair."

"You're sixty-five, George. You've worked hard. Society says you deserve a rest. You've got a pension."

"I drive the car and some kid is behind me, honkin' to hurry me up. Tonight, coming home from my last day of work ... of course, I was thinking things over, going slowly. The car behind me began to honk its horn, gun its engine, swing back and forth behind me. Damned near ran me off the road. They were just kids in a tough, dirty old car. They ripped past me. One kid leaned out the window and hollered, 'Come on, Granddad! Peel!' "

"The kids these days."

"It's not that. We were the same, I suppose."

"We never were."

"You know what gets me? We were those kids, just a few years ago. I can't understand it. It's as if we were hollerin' at ourselves to hurry up, pushin' ourselves out of the way. It doesn't make sense."

"Yes, it does."

"Boy, what a surprise those kids are in for. Just wait until, like, next Tuesday, it will seem to them, when they're being hollered at to hurry up, get out of the way. You know what I think it is? I think the world, life, goes too damned fast. It doesn't give you time to realize it's happening, here it comes, there it goes, that was it."

"If you're not busy in life, you haven't lived, either."

"You know what's been the matter with me all my life? I thought I was just great. When I was young I had the feeling I could do great things. I thought if there were advances to be made in the automotive industry, I'd be the one to make them. I thought that if this world was going to be made into a better world, I'd be the one to make it so. I certainly believed I'd be put on the executive list at Winslow Motors. I honestly thought that. And I wasn't. A man never gets over his dreams. Sure, he reaches a point where he knows the world isn't going to give him anything. But that isn't the same thing. He knows there are great men, great people in the world, people who accomplish great things, and he thinks if he can fight hard enough, long enough, he'll be one of them, he'll be great, too. That's a feeling about oneself that can take setback after setback, but it never retires."

"You've done just fine, Pop."

"At some point I realized I was on the wrong track altogether. I didn't have an education. My mind and my hands helped build one of the first cars, and now, suddenly, everyone's talking about aerodynamics. The aerodynamics of a car? Fluid transmissions. What's all that got to do with your hands? You can't figure out aerodynamics and fluid transmissions with your hands."

"There's lots you can do."

"I'll bet you that nine out of nine of your better can openers were arrived at by mathematical formulations."

"Mostly, they don't work too well. They don't really fit the hands, do you know what I mean?"

"Mother, it's really hard realizing it's all over, retiring the dream, the feeling about oneself. All week people in the office have been coming up to me and saying, 'Getting through this Saturday, eh, George?' 'Yep, boys, all through this week.' I didn't believe it. They said it, I said it, but I didn't believe it. It was just something new we were saying to each other, one more greeting, one more way of saying hello. I mean, good-bye."

"You'll see plenty of your friends from the factory, George."

"In fact, I won't. I've left their world. Their problems, their interests will continue to evolve. Soon they'll realize I don't know the details of what they're talking about. It will be too much trouble, take too much time to bring me up to date. They'll tell themselves I don't care. And, of course, I probably will care less. I've left their conversation—a conversation I've been having with them since I was a kid, Marty."

"We'll have new friends, retired people, new interests—"

"Remember that house I promised you with a servant for every wish?"

"Every woman gets promised that, George. It wouldn't have been any fun if you hadn't promised it. And we've got a fine home, George."

"Really?"

"Yes. We've made a fine home."

"Mind if I tell you something?"

"No. Go ahead."

"You'll say I'm feeling sorry for myself."

"No, I won't, Pop. Go ahead."

"Well, I left the office early tonight so I wouldn't have to stand around saying good bye. Some people are so foolish. I wasn't so bad at the office party. I still had two weeks to go. I didn't really believe I was leaving. I didn't let myself think so.

"So I went out the side way and walked around front and got into my car. But I couldn't leave. I didn't want to leave until I heard the whistle blow for the men. I never have, you know, Mother. I'm proud of that. So, like an old fool, I just sat in the car.

"There was a young girl, just a teenager, waiting in front of the door. She reminded me a lot of you. Very pretty. Very healthy. Very happy. I enjoyed just watching the little steps she took while waiting outside the door.

"Billy, the office boy, came out, and they hugged each other and kissed each other. You'd think a year had separated them, instead of just a work day. My heart swelled just watching them. They walked away very slowly, very careful of each other, arms around each other, heads leaning against each other. I watched them all the way up the street. I tried to remember what they were saying to each other.

"You don't think I'm being silly, do you?"

"No."

"And then Philip Hamilton came out."

"Which one is he?"

"He's one of the salesmen to the big distributors. A young man very much on his way up. He was wearing a nice neat suit, neat tie, clean shirt at five o'clock, one of those narrow brimmed hats. He was just what he should have been. He carried himself well, walked briskly with a little, self-confident smile on his face, like a man who makes his quota by every Friday, plays golf on Saturday, tennis on Sunday. Phil has a wife and two kids, and drives a Winslow convertible.

"The door opened again. Jim, the janitor, came out. He's an awfully nice old guy, Polish, you know. Really, he lives at the factory. No one has ever taken the trouble to retire him. His shirt was hanging out over baggy pants. He looked like he hadn't shaved since last Sunday. He tripped on the top step, barely caught himself by grabbing the railing . . . "

"Then what happened?"

"Nothing."

"That's all?"

"Yes. That's just the point. That's all."

"Well . . ."

"The whistle blew and I drove home. Those damned kids damned near ran me off the road."

"I think you're feeling sorry for yourself."

"I couldn't help wondering if Billy the office boy was promising his girl a house with a servant for every wish. And that Phil Hamilton expects to make the executive list someday. I didn't know what Jim was thinking."

"There's no point in talking about those things."

"Why not?"

"Well, there isn't, that's all. It makes you feel bad."

"No, it doesn't. It makes me feel good. It helps me to figure out what I should be thinking. You see, I didn't know what old Jim was thinking."

"Why do you care what old Jim was thinking?"

"Don't you see? I have to know what old Jim was thinking."

"No, I don't see."

"Because I want to know what I'll be thinking in a few years. Jim did catch the handrail. Will I?"

"You're being foolish."

"I told you so. I told you this was silly."

"You're not Jim any more than young Hambleton is."

"Hamilton."

"Hamilton. You're not old. Stop thinking so. Why, Paul told me the other day he's feeling old, and he's your son!"

"Thanks."

"Listen, do you want me to feel old?"

"I never felt old at Paul's age."

"Listen."

"What."

"Do you want me to feel old?"

"No, I don't."

"Then don't make me. Don't make me feel old with all your talk. I'm not old. I'm twenty-five, and nobody's telling me different."

"Okay. Then what are you doing married to someone sixty-five?"

"Well, he's young, for his age. Look at that grin! Why, I say, George, that's the grin of a toothless baby!"

" 'Toothless.' "

"Well, all right."

"All right what?"

"All right on you. If you want to feel sorry for yourself, you can. I'm going upstairs to bed."

"What do you say to a trip to Europe?"

"That would be nice."

"A trip around the world."

"We can't afford it."

"We'll go to Paris. Cheap perfume—"

"Paris."

"Cheap wine—"

"London."

"Italy. Switzerland. I've always wanted to go to Switzerland. It must be beautiful there."

"All those chocolate cows needing to be milked. That's what we can do. We can go to Switzerland and milk the cows that give chocolate milk."

"You want to be a chocolate milkmaid?"

"Skiing."

"Skiing! God! Do they have handrails in Switzerland?"

"And then Venice. The canals."

"You row."

"If I row, you'll swim."

"Probably."

"The galleries in Italy."

"At the burlesque."

"The operas. La Scala."

"I'll grumble, *basso profundo*."

"The Isle of Capri."

"I want to go to Africa. Big game hunting."

"Shoot things?"

"Of course shoot things. Lions. Elephants."

"Door to door salesmen."

"Sure, we'll bag a salesman or two. Talk Swahili with the Masai."

"They play bridge?"

"Poker. With their spears. We'll go traipsing over the hills to-gether—"

"What will I wear?"

"No, really. How about it? Would you like to take a trip?"

"Where?"

"We could get in the car and tour New England. How about California? We could go peek behind the movie screen, see how they enlarge all those people out there."

"You've been driving all your life."

"We can drive that new aerodynamic Winslow right into the ground. See who gives out first, the latest Winslow, or the oldest Winslow maker."

"I don't know, Pop. The Winslow's a pretty good car . . . "

"One hundred and sixty-five horsepower. God, we started with nine, I think."

"It would be snowy in New England, anyway."

"We could go up to Columbia Falls. You've never been there."

"You said you'd never go back."

"When?"

"When you went up there in the thirties."

"Oh. Yeah. Well, we could go up there again. None of the old folks would still be up there."

"Why did you say you didn't want to go back?"

"Oh, I don't know. Another case of punctured pride, I guess. Punctured something."

"You've been a proud man."

"I've been punctured enough, too."

"What were you proud about that time?"

"Oh, I don't know. Myself, I guess. I couldn't take you that time, remember? You were working on that school play with Barbara."

"That's right."

"Barbara was playing a tree in Sherwood Forest, or something."

"I had to make a lot of costumes. Elms, oaks, and pines."

"Costumes, yeah. I had to go up to that hand tool exposition, or whatever it was, in Portland. And I went up to Columbia Falls."

"You were only there a day."

"Only a few hours. You know that old fellow, Higgins? No? I thought I must have talked about him. Maybe I haven't. Well, when I was a boy all he talked about was sheep. He owned a sheep farm.

He never would let anybody talk about anything, except his sheep. He had a big ewe, McAdoo, and all he'd talk about, when he wasn't talking about his other sheep, was his big ewe, McAdoo. But I liked the old man. He was a nice old guy. I liked him the way you do sometimes, when you're a kid.

"While I was up there, I thought I'd drop in on him, just to see if he was alive and kicking. This was even before I went back to the farm I was brought up on. I drove into his driveway—I had the Winslow roadster in those days, remember?—I drove into his drive-way, wondering if he'd recognize me. Sure enough, there he was, down the driveway, standing in front of one of his pens.

"All of a sudden he started gesturing madly and screaming at me. Then I saw a little lamb dart across the dirt driveway in front of me. I couldn't have hit him if I'd tried.

" 'By God, you almost hit him, George.'

"So he remembered me. 'How are you, old goat?'

" 'Fine, George, fine. But you really hadn't ought to drive that way. There's lots of livestock around here. Sam Jenkins lost a calf last week by one of you drivers.'

" 'You don't have a motor yet, eh?'

" 'No, and I never will have. They ought to be taken off the roads. Bad for the livestock. Nothing worse. Mow 'em down like wheat.'

" 'Well, how you been?'

" 'I lost a lamb, too, you know.'

" 'That so?'

" 'A year ago. Right up there on the road. Ran him right down. Nothing we could save. What kind of a car is that, anyway, George?'

" 'Winslow.'

" 'Never have one of those. It's getting so you can't cross the road to your own mailbox without having to watch.'

" 'You should watch.'

" 'You know, when my father came up here—that was a lot of years ago, boy—when my father came up here—you won't believe this, but it's true—we used to be able to let sheep run loose all over the place. They'd roam way up there over the ridge, cross the road twenty times a day, if they took a notion to. Never lost one of them, save for their own stupidity. Now we're having to pen 'em in close as the minister's daughter. Sam Jenkins lost a crittur last week by one of them things. Run him right over. What business you in now, anyway, boy?'

" 'Automobiles.'

" 'Sell 'em, or build 'em?'

" 'Build 'em.' Help build 'em.'

" 'George? That ain't helpin'. That's hinderin'. Well, I'm goin' to make sure there's nothin' up on the road before you take that thing out of here. Back her around slowly, now, George, like I say. Wait until I see if the way is clear.'

"He went up the driveway ahead of me onto the road, held me back with his hand until he had stretched his neck both ways, then waved me on.

"I waved back at him."

"Did he see you?"

"No. He'd gone back down the driveway. To his sheep."

"What did you expect, Pop?"

"He recognized me. That's more than I expected, after all those years."

"That's pretty good."

"Might be better if he hadn't. Guess I wanted something from him. I don't know what. Maybe real recognition. I don't know. Whatever it was, I didn't get it."

"He just didn't know how else to act."

"Then I went on up to the farm.

"You know, Mother, when you're an orphan and someone takes you in, you're mighty grateful. It means you know where you are eating and sleeping for a while. I was grateful. The folks at the farm gave me love. At least, I thought so. When you're young I guess you can take anything as love, if you want it badly enough. I worked hard for them, growing up. Anyway, things had worked out, and I felt at home there. It was the only place I ever had really, and they were the only folks.

"After I left there, I used to write letters to the farm. At first, I'd suggest coming back on a trip, for a weekend, or a week. I wanted to know how they were doin'. I never, never got an answer.

"Anyway, once a year, around Christmas, I would still write them, never fail, telling them where I was, how I was doing, asking them how they were doing.

"Never an answer.

"Well, I drove into the yard. Ed came out onto the steps of the house. He had grown very fat.

" 'Is that George?' he said.

" 'That's George, Ed,' I answered.

" 'Teeny!' he called into the house. 'It's George Brice!'

"I went up the steps to shake his hand. He barely gave me his hand. His overalls smelled foul.

"This terrible looking, fat woman came to the door and peered at me from behind the screen. She didn't say anything.

"Ed said, 'Where you been all these years, George?' There was something really odd in his eyes. Scared, maybe.

" 'Well, I been busy, Ed. I been busy.'

" 'You met the Missus? Come here, Teeny. Meet George Brice.'

"She nodded from behind the screen door, a strand of hair falling down her face. 'Afternoon.'

" 'Would you like some coffee, George? We're just havin' some apple pie.'

" 'Love some.'

"He brought me through the door into the warm, homey kitchen. Everything smelled of apple pie. There was the same wooden table with the knife scars on it, the four chairs, now very shaky, the old iron gas stove. Everything was as it had been, only older, and dirtier.

"We sat around the wooden table. It smelled faintly of dishwater. Teeny cut me a piece of pie, and Ed poured me some coffee.

" 'What happened to the folks, Ed?'

" 'Gee, George, they're all gone. I thought you knew that.'

" 'I never heard. Even the old man?'

" 'A sack of grain fell on him from the loft in the barn when he was bendin' over. Sent his head against the sharp edge of a plow.'

" 'That's too bad.'

" 'The old Missus found him. They guessed he'd never regained consciousness. Bled to death.'

" 'What was a sack of grain doing up in the loft?'

" 'New man left it there, on the weak board. Didn't know any better.'

" 'The old Missus gone, too?'

" 'Ayuh. She was very old. Closed her eyes during the night.'

" 'When was that?'

" 'Oh, 'bout five, six years ago. They're all gone. Teeny and me took care of the old Missus till she died. It was some four years she was invalid.'

" 'I didn't know you were married, Ed.'

" 'You been away a long time, boy.'

" 'Congratulations. Best wishes.'

" 'You married?'

" 'Long time ago.'

" 'Got any kids?'

" 'Two. Boy and a girl.'

" 'They like the country?'

" 'Guess so. Paul talks about wanting a dog. You and Teeny don't have any?'

" 'Sure. Just had a litter come out.'

" 'I mean, kids.'

" 'Oh, no. It's too much on us, if you know what I mean. I mean, with the place and all.'

" 'Sure.'

" 'Hard enough, 'round here. More pie?'

" 'No, thanks.'

" 'Gee, it's good to see you, George.'

" 'It's good to be back.'

" 'Thinking of coming back?'

" 'No. I'd never do that.'

" 'Me and Teeny been wondering all these years. There was some question when the old Missus died.'

" 'Oh?'

" 'We don't want no trouble, George.'

" 'Trouble?'

" 'I mean, you with that new car out there, and all.'

" 'I don't get you, Ed.'

" 'Well, you see, the old Missus left us this place in her will.'

" 'Well, I guess you were pretty good to her."

" 'That's what we figure. But the will has never been sure because she never mentioned you in it.'

" 'Why should she?'

" 'You were adopted, George. They had to adopt you, 'cause you were younger, to get work out of you.'

" 'I see.'

" 'Me, they had to hire on, 'cause I was older. It's that simple.'

" 'Oh.'

" 'The old judge here in town said we couldn't be sure. You might come back any time, he said, and make trouble, because you were adopted, George.'

" 'That's right. Yes. I know.'

" 'I mean, I wasn't adopted, if that's the way you want to look at it, but that's just because I was older. At least, that's the way I figure.'

" 'Yes, I guess that's right.'

" 'And I've stuck close by all these years. I could have gone off, too, and gotten myself a fancy motor car, but I stuck by. I've done my share around here. And when the old man passed away, I was the only one the old Missus had to lean on.'

" 'Yes, that's right.'

" 'And, you know, she said that if I took care of her all the days of her life and saw that she got a proper burial the farm would be mine. Me and Teeny's. Sort of a bargain, you know. And she put it in the will. That was what she wanted. The farm was hers, you know.'

" 'That's right, Ed. That's right.'

" 'So the way I figure it, George, you don't really have a claim to it, George.'

" 'No, Ed, I don't have a claim to it. It's yours.'

" 'Well, that's what I figure. I mean, where the old Missus said. And the farm was hers to start with.'

" 'That's right, Ed. Still grow potatoes, I see.'

" 'Yes, though I've had to let some of the fields go. It's not the way it was when there was you and the old man around.'

" 'I guess not. Well, I guess I better start back.'

" 'Okay, George, well, it was good to see you.'

" 'It was good to see you, too, Ed. You haven't changed a bit.'

"The farm had changed. A lot of it had gone to weed. Needed paint. I was never cold there, as a boy, and that's cold country. It was summer when I was there in the thirties, but you know, as I drove out of the yard, I'll be damned if I didn't feel cold."

"You must have been pretty disappointed, Pop."

"I remember shivering in the car."

"They were glad to see you, but for all the wrong reasons."

"They were glad to see me go."

"They had worried about you for years."

"They had my address. They could have written, or had 'the old judge' write."

"They'd rather worry about you than confront you. Maybe you never would show up."

"Doesn't every man want to go home someday and let the folks see how well he's done?"

"Those who have gone away. Those people you found still up in Columbia Falls had never gone away. They couldn't understand. They saw you and your Winslow roadster as just a threat to them."

"And to their sheep. I felt I never wanted to go back up there."

"You want to go back there now?"

"No."

"All right. We won't."

"Everything's changed."

"Well, I guess that has to happen. Just like can openers."

"To hell with can openers."

"You want to tour California?"

"Do you?"

"Santa Barbara. The land of flowers. It never rains in Santa Barbara."

"How do the flowers grow?"

"Somebody must have invented something."

"Somebody invented a formula."

"San Francisco."

"Hills, ugh. You can go up them. I'll stick to going down them."

"Los Angeles. Beverly Hills. Hollywood."

"Once ... "

"What?"

"Once I would have walked to Hollywood to see a movie star."

"You're kidding."

"I kid you not."

"Any star in particular?"

"Mae West."

"I don't believe it."

"Greta Garbo."

"George, really ... "

"Don't worry. I never could walk it now."

"Shall I buy you a bike?"

"Who are these people we pay so much to act out our fantasies for us? What do they look like in person? Do they really exist? Are they alive and the rest of us only half alive?"

"George, you're talking crazy. You've never even gone to the movies that much."

"Everyone's a little bit crazy. Crazy sometimes. Remember when I was turning forty-eight?"

"Let's not talk about that."

"You know what I'm talking about though, don't you?"

"Ancient history."

"At our age, Marty, what isn't ancient history?"

"Over. Done with. Forgotten."

"It's not, you know. I was thinking about it the other day. I was wondering if you ever really understood."

"Of course I did."

"I don't believe you did."

"I did."

"I think you were just being nice about it. Practical, you know what I mean?"

"No, I understood. It was difficult, but I understood."

"You never did anything like that to me."

"How do you know?"

"You didn't."

"Well, I could have, easily enough."

"I'm sure. But you didn't."

"No."

"I would have walked out on me for that. Maybe you should have."

"No, Pop."

"I did a not-very-nice thing to you. But I did it late, you know, if that's saying anything for myself. Late, and once. I didn't rush into it. And that was after years of confusion."

"George, I don't need to hear this. It's all right."

"It's not all right. It's not all right with me, yet."

"What do you mean, with you?"

"At first, I thought I was being ignored. I thought I was being ignored after Paul was born."

"Now what do you mean? I never ignored you."

"No. Of course not."

"What do you mean?"

"I just didn't fit much into your schedule."

"What schedule? I found my reality in the children. You found your reality in building Winslow cars. I never had a schedule."

"You did, in fact. In the morning, I'd want to talk to you about the day, whatever I was nervous about, and you'd be washing their noses and sending them off to school."

"Raising children is a serious business."

"I know. I'd try to help. Now you tell me I was cute. Laughable. Building the Winslow car was a serious business. Keeping us all sheltered and fed was serious."

"You were cute."

"I'd come home, and you'd be feeding the baby. I'd come in here to the den and recount the day to myself. I'd want to go to bed and you'd be bathing the baby. I'd go to bed and dream dreams about the future, not sure who was in it."

"Isn't that the way it's supposed to work?"

"Of course."

"You know what?"

"What?"

"We were jealous of each other."

"I guess so."

"Jealous of each other's time and energy, attention, being given to other things: the children, work, whatever. Survival."

"That's love."

"That's love."

"When I was in my forties I realized I could do anything in one day Paul could do. I could put in a full work day, then play eighteen holes of golf, attend a business cocktail party, take you to dinner, the theater, dance until two in the morning. The difference was, I couldn't get up and do it again the next day, or the next . . . or the next . . . . It's the recuperative powers that get old . . . . I'll be honest with you. Okay if I'm honest with you?"

"I guess you're determined to be."

"When I was a kid, before I married you, every morning, of course, I awoke excited. That was natural. Some days I would awake convinced that if I didn't make love to a woman that day I would go nuts. I would go crazy. There would be no way I could return to bed at night if I had not made love to a woman, or committed myself to an asylum for the about-to-be-criminally insane."

"Was it that strong for you?"

"Absolutely."

"George, I've never featured you as a rapist. Although I do remember you returning from a few business trips . . . "

"It was that bad. Or good. And the morning came when I didn't wake up excited. At first I didn't care. In fact, I was a bit relieved. Then there came a lot of days, one after the other, in which I didn't wake up excited. There hasn't been enough protein in my diet, I told myself. I've been working too hard; I'm too concerned about my work. But I also knew that a few months before I'd try to think about my work and find myself thinking about sex. I'd get excited at the most awkward times, in the most awkward places. Suddenly, I found myself trying to think about sex and finding myself thinking about my work. And I didn't think that was terribly funny. All your life you don't think your hormones govern what you think. Then you discover, they do. And to a certain extent, they always have."

"Did you go to a doctor?"

"I didn't say I went to a doctor."

"I went to a doctor. I couldn't understand how you could lose interest in me so suddenly. I dieted. It seemed so sudden."

"Well. I've never been sure a marriage can survive the forties. I mean, really survive it. If a husband and wife survive their forties together, they must have made peace with each other. But not without their friendship undergoing some mighty big changes."

"Their forties, their twenties, their thirties, their fifties."

"I didn't know you went to a doctor. I thought I was having all the feelings."

"He told me the clocks of men and women are set differently. That's an element of time people seldom realize. It sure makes for a lot of grief."

"I'm sorry. I'm really sorry, Marty."

"It's all over with now. I don't even remember her name."

"I do. It was Clare."

"I didn't even remember."

"You're a good sport."

"It's those clocks. Time. There are so many different kinds of clocks in our lives. You ask me if I understand. No one can really understand time."

"The hell with clocks. I would have walked out."

"It was a long time ago. Seventeen years."

"Not long enough. It will never be long enough. You remember how I acted at the office party with Clare? I left you out in the cold."

"Nonsense."

"It's the dreams, you see. Reality corrects the dreams, but does not kill them. Forty-eight years old, almost fifty, not quite. I kept patting my pockets, wondering what I'd forgotten. I'd been going through the same routine every day, week, month, for years, and that hit me between the eyes. I went to the market for food; to bed before eleven. I slept late on Sunday mornings. What had I missed? How much time had I left? Why was I giving Cary Grant dollars to charm other ladies for me? I was getting pudgy, growing a second chin. I was envying Paul, my own son, if you'd believe it, his clean limbs, his energy.

"It became impractical to dream any more, but, still, I did. I caught myself holding my stomach in while I was shaving. At the office I found I couldn't remember the specifications of every car on the road, every piece of machinery in the world any more. There wasn't as much reason to care. Younger men were getting promoted over me. The girls in the office were watching them. If they noticed me at all as a person, the women said I reminded them of their fathers.

"Then, one did notice me as a person. Clare flirted with me, flirted seriously. Winked at me in the hall, stood close to me and asked my advice on every little thing. I never knew why. For a while there, I had myself convinced I attracted her. I took her to lunch. We didn't

talk of kids and camps and cars. We talked of champagne and châ-
teaux and charm."

"Her hair was bleached. Badly bleached."

"She gave me a gift of time. What else can I say? For a few
months she let me keep the dream that there was a future, that
there was time, more than enough time."

"There were the clocks. All those nights you came home so late
from the office and told me you were working on the new plant in
New Jersey. I knew."

"When I was away, helping to set up the new plant in New Jersey?
I said I was alone."

"You were alone."

"I wasn't. I worked it so Clare could come with me."

"You said you were alone."

"I lied."

"Oh. And all that time I told myself you were away from me, but
you were also away from Clare."

"Why didn't you check up, Martha? It would have been easy. All
you needed to do was—"

"You said you were in New Jersey alone."

"I would have been happy to have been caught. It wouldn't have
meant so much through these years. You should have checked up
on me. You were too damned good. What was to keep me from
going out and doing it again, doing it continuously?"

"You didn't."

"No. I didn't."

"You did it once, as far as I know."

"I had to do it that once. Does that make sense? I never gave up
my dreams, at least, without a fight. With Clare I was fighting for
some dream of myself that was going fast, too fast. It wasn't anything I was doing against you. This may sound funny, but it had
nothing to do with you, Marty."

"I think I knew that."

"I just wanted to tell you about it. I wanted to make sure you
knew."

"I didn't know. Not about those months in New Jersey."

"Do you think I should have told you?"

"I don't know. No, maybe not."

"I've thought about it."

"It was better not to know ... "

"Are you upset now?"

"No. You came back from New Jersey much more at peace with yourself. I thought it was because the new plant was a success. There never really has been anything come between us, George. A few bears in the woods, and occasionally we've had to fight for each other with our backs to each other ... "

"Maybe you feel hurt that after I did such a stupid thing I lied about it for so long."

"No, I'm glad you did."

"You are?"

"I've always loved your pride, George. I've never punctured it."

"Were you jealous?"

"*Furiously!*"

"You were?"

"*Furiously!*"

"That's good. You weren't seeing me as a romantic figure anymore, you know. As a lover."

"What do you think I was seeing you as?"

"Family errand boy in funny pants."

"I thought you just said your little affair with Clare had nothing to do with me, wasn't *against* me?"

"It wasn't. It was for you."

"Beg pardon?"

"You saw me differently when I came back from New Jersey. You treated me differently."

"But I didn't know Clare was in New Jersey with you."

"Come on, Marty. You suspected it."

"Yes. I did."

"You see? We've both been lying."

"I was glad to have you back."

"I was glad to be back. You know something else?"

"Not sure I want to."

"All the time I was with Clare, almost all the time, I was thinking about you. Isn't that ridiculous?"

"Ridiculous."

"I wanted to tell Marty this, show Marty that. The whole affair with Clare became quite a bore."

"I thought it might."

"I'm sorry, Martha."

"Say, 'I'm sorry, Marty.' "

"I'm sorry, Marty. Okay?"

"The fact that this has bothered us for seventeen years shows how innocent we are."

"Okay. Now, where do you want to go? South America? We could learn to samba."

"Grow coffee."

"And listen to the church bell?"

"Is that what old folks do in South America?"

"They listen to the church bell. And tend the grandchildren."

"How many grandchildren do you have to have to be in the 'in' group?"

"I doubt we qualify."

"Isn't that terrible? We had two children and each of our children has two children."

"We're nice, little, self-disciplined Americans."

"Let's see. Paul's been married ten years, and Barbara, four. She might have more."

"She married late, though. She had to go to New York to have a career first."

"I'm glad she did."

"Nonsense."

"No, I'm glad she did. It gave her self-reliance."

"Right. So every little thing that goes wrong with her marriage will cause her to remember her independence, how well she got along without husband and babies."

"It's not like that."

"I'm glad you never worked. Our home would have been on the rocks years ago."

"I don't think so. Barbara's a good person. She'll make the best of things, poor dear."

"Why did you say 'poor dear'?"

"I didn't."

"You did. You said 'poor dear.' "

"Well, I meant for them to have two children in the first four years of their married life."

"Oh."

"No. He's a lovely fellow."

"Who said anything about him?"

"Well, you did."

"No, I didn't. I haven't said one word about Chet."

"There, you just did."

"That's not fair!"

"Well, I mean, Chet's a fine fellow, and I think Barbara will make the best of it."

"Now what does that mean?"

"I mean, I'm glad they're a happily married couple. Period."

"Want to know something?"

"What?"

"I don't like him either."

"No!"

"What a jerk!"

"Pop!"

"Can't tell who's the man and who's the woman in that family. The matter seems up for continuous debate and negotiation."

"I didn't know you'd noticed."

"Haven't you noticed how I don't love to go to their house for dinner? 'I'll make the drinks.' 'No, I'll make the drinks.' Who the hell wants a drink badly enough to listen to an argument about who makes it? 'Chet! There are lumps in this whipped potato!' Oh, God. Their dinner conversation seldom ascends above a moving discussion about who vacuumed the living room rug."

"Why didn't you tell me? We could have had some great laughs about it. Or tears."

"Tears. Right. There just isn't time in family life to negotiate every little thing. There come too many times when everyone has to know who he is, know his responsibilities, and just act accordingly, without a lot of talk. What are they going to do in a crisis? Decide then who is going to bundle the bleeding baby in a blanket and who is going to get the car to go to the hospital? I worry about them."

"George, I cried at their wedding. I mean, really cried."

"I know you did. I never loved you more."

"Chet just doesn't seem a very solid man. You know what I mean? He just doesn't seem very definite, sure of himself."

"He lets our daughter get away with way too much."

"It's none of our business, of course. Now."

"We only raised her."

"You know, Pop, there was a time when I was sure our children hated us."

"Not hatred. Just a slow, burning contempt."

"I could never understand why. We're perfectly nice people."

"Yes, we are. Perfectly nice."

"Yet they hated us."

"It was awkward. Doing everything in the world, from going to work in the morning to cleaning the garage, over and over again, for these short people who deigned to speak to us only when they needed extra cash."

"It was awkward for them, too. I suppose we couldn't stop treating them like children. We were trying to restrain Paul and Barbara in diapers while they were trying to restrain themselves in a jock strap and bra. I read, once during that period—"

"Oh, did you read, too?"

"Volumes."

"I spent most Saturday afternoons in the public library."

"I read that children hate their parents at a particular age because they have been weak before them."

"The parents?"

"No, the children. They have been helpless, mewling and puking creatures, and in order to develop a new image of themselves they have to reject the people who first saw them that way, their parents."

"Yes, that's right. I remember that one now. It was a big, red book—"

"With a gold embossed title. I don't remember the title."

"*Breaking the Egg* I think that one was called."

"That's right. *Breaking the Egg*. I had my own copy. You didn't need to go to the library."

"Well, they got over it. Or we did."

"Still. It was a surprise when Barbara brought Chester home from New York."

"Paul used to bring home stray dogs."

"Just the same way. I felt like saying, 'Barbara, put that Chester back where you found him this instant! Someone may want him.' Isn't that awful?"

"It's about time we were awful. And after they were married they used to make those stiff little calls. Suggest I ought to help you more around the house."

"Did they? Barbara told me I should go fishing with you."

"God! How did we ever make it on our own!"

"Chet's taken to advising me on my magazine subscriptions. Did you know that? Recommends something called *Silver Streak Travels.*"

"And Paul would want me to dandle his baby on my knee. There is a time to dandle, and a time to watch a limited amount of dandling from the comfort and security of a dry easy chair across the room. Isn't that from Ecclesiastes?"

"I think so."

"That child got the shortest dandlings from me."

"But they are wonderful."

"Who?"

"The children."

"Oh, yes. They're wonderful, all right. Raised them myself. Wouldn't want any others."

"Good people."

"That's right. Good people."

"I suppose that during those years we knew we liked them as small children, but we weren't sure if we liked them as people."

"I held my breath in suspense. Did you notice how blue in the face I was during those years?"

"Well, they've turned into nice people."

"I like them."

"You know, Paul's coming over tomorrow."

"He is?"

"He and Margot. They're having some problems with Paul, Junior in school. Wanted to talk with the grandfolks about it."

"Are we complimented?"

"Oh, Margot's come to me often."

"She has?"

"Margot's a nice person. You ought to stop greeting her like someone you met last week at a cocktail party."

"Why, I feel left out, I do."

"What do you know about raising children?"

"I was one once. Besides that, I watched you raise two."

"Well, they're coming tomorrow."

"Now that I'm retired, sound advice is expected of me?"

"You can even do your fair share of dandling."

"All right. But I won't make faces. Positively."

"Do you think we loved our children too much?"

"What do you mean by that? They were never spoiled. Too spoiled."

"Oh, I don't know. It just seemed at times we loved them more than they could ever love us. We seemed to have *had* love for them, somehow, while their love ... oh, I don't know ... somehow has always seemed judgmental, conditional, somehow, something for which we've had to keep working, striving ... "

"They'll love their children."

"Yes, I guess so."

"Maybe they'll do better than we did. Who knows?"

"They couldn't. You were always there for them, George, solid, certain—"

"And sometimes right?"

"A father shouldn't be right all the time. Just solidly *there*."

"He can't be there, you know, unless the mother points him out, once in a while."

"You've given us a fine home—"

"—not filled with satins and silks, marble and gold, however it went—"

"—educated them both, through college."

"Had to. I was in that plant forty-five years and never made the executive list because I didn't have a college degree. What you know means nothing, anymore; only what people say you know: it's all just so much paper."

"You've done well. I hope they do as well."

"I wonder if they think we're awfully old."

"Who?"

"The children."

"Oh, I suppose so. They always have."

"Old and decrepit. We will be soon enough."

"Hush. You know what Paul said."

"What did Paul say?"

"He said that each age has its own beauty."

"Original fellow. Did he pat you on your arm as he said it?"

"No, but he smiled. I think he meant it. Each age does have its own beauty. I think it's true."

"Maybe. As long as people don't give us purple, button-up sweaters. I wouldn't like you in purple, Mother."

"You have to bring the laundry down to Turner's tomorrow."

"What about the man who picks it up?"

"I find these new laundromats much cheaper. As long as you're free ... "

"Oh, yes. I almost forgot."

"You've got to be here when Paul and Margot arrive."

"Do you think they'll bring us purple sweaters?"

"The fire is dying out."

"It's nice, isn't it? The room seems smaller. The world seems smaller now. I'm glad to be alone with you once again. I mean, really alone. Nothing between us: no children, no work, no noise, no hurry, no bother."

"It is nice, isn't it?"

"You know, a man is alone with his wife very few times during his lifetime. I'm just discovering that tonight. It's nice spending time with you again, Marty."

"And with you, George."

"Shall we go to bed now?"

"I'm comfortable here. Snugly."

"Marty, thank you very much."

"For what?"

"For everything."

"Thank you, George."

"Let's go upstairs."

"All right. We should do something with the fire."

"It's all right. It will die down."

SATCHELS AND SNAILS

Chambeau opened his eyes. From his bed he saw his school books piled on the desk across the room. A model airplane, only half supported, was perched on the top book. Its nose pointed toward the surface of the desk.

The young pilot, of course, stood shamefaced between the desk and the bed, waiting to be reprimanded. Chambeau glared at him. "That was a bad landing, Mister."

"Yes, sir."

"Where did you learn to fly, anyway? Out of the comics?"

Chambeau felt he had been hard enough on the young pilot. Anyone can make a bad landing.

"All right, Mister. Report to mess. Hereafter be more careful of government property."

"Come on, Chum," his mother said from the hall door. She was going back downstairs to the kitchen. "Up, up, up."

"I'm up, up, up."

He got out of bed, stepping on a pile of airplane and rocket picture cards. He had been going through them last night, before he went to sleep.

He looked sleepily at the bright young orderly standing before him. "Have they shot the dirty traitors yet?"

"No, General Chambeau. Your orders were to have morning parade first and then shoot them."

"I forgot that."

Chambeau went to the open window and looked out. First there was the parade. In the morning there was always the parade. The marshal waited for Chambeau to appear at the window. He raised his baton and blew his whistle. Immediately there was the sound of the bugles and the rat-tat-tat of the drums. Then the red-jacketed soldiers marched past in lines four abreast. All their faces were serious and their eyes were straight ahead. They held their naked swords up against their shoulders. The sword points reached halfway up the soldiers' fur hats. There were many lines of these soldiers. They marched stiffly and perfectly. Chambeau stood in his window, watching them. He felt pride in his men. There was a sharp order and the soldiers stopped. Another order and they faced the window. Another order and the band played *Hail to the Chief*. When the music stopped Chambeau saluted the soldiers and then they marched in quick-time back to their barracks.

"Very good," Chambeau said to the orderly.

The orderly, braced in his tunic, had been standing behind Chambeau.

"Yes, sir. Thank you, sir."

Chambeau pointed through the window. "What's that dog doing there on the parade ground?" he demanded.

"Dog, sir?"

Chambeau leaned through the window. "Out of there, Skip! Out!"

The dog looked up from the garbage bucket near the garage and wagged its tail. "Hi, Skip! How are you, boy. Here, Skip! Here, Skip!"

His father looked into the bedroom. "Aren't you ready, yet?"

Chambeau turned from the window. "I'm up."

"Well, put your pants on. It's breakfast time." He started downstairs. "Come on, son."

"Orderly, have that dog shot."

"Yes, sir."

Chambeau turned toward the window again.

A line of ragged, half-starved prisoners were led staggering into the yard. Messy beards did not conceal the scars and welts on their faces. They were bound together by their wrists. Wildly desperate eyes glanced again and again up at Chambeau as the prisoners stumbled along. They were lined up against the wall. The soldiers in battle dress with rifles, the firing squad, lined up facing the prisoners. Saying nothing, the prisoners shot their eyes back and forth from the firing squad to Chambeau standing in his window.

"Shoot them," said Chambeau.

The orderly held his arm up.

The field sergeant said, "Ready. Aim. Fire!"

The rifle reports were instantaneous.

The prisoners' legs collapsed beneath them.

It was a successful shooting. All dead.

"Very good," said Chambeau.

"Yes, sir. Thank you, sir."

"Hey, you up there! Hurry up." His father stood at the bottom of the stairs.

"I'm coming."

Charley came into the room. He was a fat man in a sweatshirt. He chewed a cigar.

"Hiya, boy!"

"Hi, Charley."

The wet cigar went from one corner of Charley's mouth to the other.

"How are ya, boy? You all set for the big bout?"

Chambeau made light of it. Ten rounds isn't much. He had gone ten rounds many times. And always won.

"I was just over watchin' Rocky gettin' rubbed. He looks scared, Chambeau. Real scared."

"He should."

"He'll never take the championship from you. Never in a million years. You'll rub him out."

"Might as well give the kid a chance," Chambeau said. "They all deserve a chance."

"Sure, you'll rub him out. You'll rub 'em all out."

Charley helped Chambeau dress.

Chambeau had a new one-two knockout combination he had devised himself. No one could stand up against it. So far he had used the new combination to beat John L. Sullivan, Joe Louis, Rocky Marciano, Floyd Patterson, Mohammed Ali, Marvin Hagler and the Italian contender, Mark S. Anthony.

Charley waited for him by the door of the dressing room. They were going down to the weighing-in. There he would see this new Rocky and see just how scared he was. If Rocky looked too scared, Chambeau would say something kind to him. Rocky would need courage to climb into the ring with him.

Chambeau and his manager walked down the hotel stairs. Charley's hand was on Chambeau's shoulder. Of course there were crowds in the lobby waiting for him. The men from the press with tickets in their hatbands took pictures of him and said, "How you feel,

Champ?" Many people came forward wtih autograph books and Chambeau stopped and signed each one. It took them a long time to cross the lobby.

He went into the kitchen.

From the stove, his mother said, "Hurry with your cereal, dear. Your egg is ready."

His father looked away from the morning television news and said, "Where, may I ask, have you been?"

"I'd rather have steak," Chambeau said, sliding to his place along the breakfast nook bench.

"Do you have to take all morning to get dressed?"

"I had a great many things to do."

"Didn't you finish your homework last night?"

"Of course," Chambeau lied. It would be a bad day in school. All days were.

His mother said, "He's just sleepy. Early to bed for you tonight."

"Oh, no."

"Oh, yes."

"Please oh, no. I'm not sleepy, honest."

"Please oh, yes."

She sounded too firm.

"I won't come home," Chambeau said. "Then you can't make me go to bed early. I'll sleep in the creek bed so I'll be able to stay up as late as I want."

It might be a good idea to sleep in the creek bed anyway.

His father asked, "Why would anyone in a creek bed want to stay up late?"

"Don't be difficult. I mean: Sir."

His mother sat at the table. She looked at his father with hatred. Chambeau saw the look. He saw it every morning. He glanced at his father out of the corner of his eye. On his father's face was contempt for such a look. He saw that every morning, too. Then there was the look of confusion, hurt and fear, on his mother's face. These looks passed between his parents every morning as they all sat down at the kitchen table for breakfast together.

Chambeau's Indian friend, No Rain Today, stood at the edge of the forest and barked three times like a coyote.

Chambeau went out to him.

"How!" he said.

"How!" No Rain Today answered.

"What's up, No Rain Today?"

"Chief Too Many Wives make much trouble. He burnumed many ranches during the night. Many brave warriors come here."

Chambeau spat tobacco juice on the ground.

He said, "No Rain Today, Chief Too Many Wives much bad medicine. We make stop to him."

"That's why I come tell you," No Rain Today said.

No Rain Today had Chambeau's horse saddled, ready for him, just inside the forest.

Together they rode through the forest together, Chambeau and No Rain Today, horses galloping, white manes and white tails spread in the wind of their riding. They skirted the big trees and jumped the shrubs. Straight-backed they leaned backward in their saddles going down the hills. They leaned forward, their cheeks almost against the horses' necks going up the hills. These were the fastest horses in the West. Still, it was a far piece to ride. Chambeau felt the rawness as his lungs were stretched to their limits. The people in the towns and the Indian villages stared as Chambeau and No Rain Today rode through on their white horses in the early morning. The people knew Chambeau and No Rain Today were brave and strong and good, and they loved them.

His father said, "You're not eating your egg."

"I don't like my egg," Chambeau answered.

"There are millions of children in Ethiopia who would give their right arms to have an egg like that."

In fact, the television had just showed millions of children starving in Ethiopia.

"I don't need any more right arms. I've got a whole case of 'em upstairs."

Chambeau grinned at his mother, but she was pouring herself more coffee and looking distracted.

"Come on, eat up," she said. "You'll be hungry by eleven o'clock."

"I'll be hungry by eleven o'clock anyway. That's when I have Geography. What's the leading export from Brazil? Chocolate nut sundaes!"

"I'll put your breakfast egg in a bag for you to eat at lunch time. That's all."

"Oh, no."

"Oh, yes."

"Please oh, no."

"All right. I'll give you your lunch if you eat your breakfast."

"You're a pal," he said.

While Chambeau was eating his egg, his mother and father talked about getting the car fixed. A little joke passed between them. Then his father said something about the way she spent money. She said something about his always being able to work late at night to earn overtime. Then they each poured more coffee for themselves and were silent over their cups.

Chambeau stood up from his finished egg.

"Off to school," his father said.

"You mean, today isn't a beach day? Really?"

Chambeau found his school books on the kitchen counter. He couldn't remember bringing them downstairs.

"Kiss me?" his mother said. She glanced at her husband as she raised her face to her son.

"Okay, doll baby. Pucker up."

He and his mother laughed. He kissed her on the cheek.

"See you later, doll baby. I'll pick you up about eight."

"Your hat. It's October."

"I don't need my hat."

His father said, "Wear your hat."

The orderly said, "Have you your hat, sir? Your swagger stick? Very good, sir."

"Okay. I've got my hat."

"Good. Do well in school today."

"Right. Sure. Of course."

His bicycle was leaning against the back porch railing.

The mechanic was just finishing up. He wore his baseball cap backwards on his head.

"She all right?" Chambeau asked.

"You mean to take her up?"

"Yes."

"We've patched her up as good as we can. You brought her back from yesterday's mission with maybe a few too many holes in her."

"Ventilation," Chambeau said. "In a dogfight you need a little ventilation."

"Yes, sir."

Chambeau looked at the sky. It was overcast. Looked like a high pressure area in the middle east. "Well," he said. "Let's rev the old crate up. See if she's good for one more mission."

He got onto his bicycle and spun the pedals backwards.

The engine spluttered but it sounded okay. He waved at the mechanic through the windshield to remove the blocks from in front of the wheels.

Chambeau taxied onto the runway.

"Chambeau to tower. Chambeau to tower. I'm taking off."

"Tower to Chambeau. Tower to Chambeau. Roger. Happy hunting. Over. Out."

Chambeau gunned the engine, accelerated quickly. The engine roared as it pulled him down the field.

Chambeau was on his way to school.

At the kitchen table, his mother finished her third cup of coffee. She said, "I guess it's worth it, for his sake, staying together a little while longer."

"Yes," his father said. "We'll wait until he is twelve years old."

QUICK IN QUARREL

1

It did not snow until the next day, but all that day there was the smell of snow.

That day there was the quiet, sluggish progress of the line of soldiers through fields new to them. The grass was tall and the ground was wet. The soldiers sauntered onward, looking through the grass at the ground for mines, and looking across the field at each other to the right and to the left to confirm again and again that they all were going forward. The helmets on their heads, the rifles in their hands, the packs hanging from their shoulders, the grenades hanging from their belts put the burden of their weight on the hips of the young soldiers. In the field that day there was the quiet, sauntering progress of the line of young soldiers.

And there was the fear.

Dan Prescott sauntered along with the rest of them. The mud was squishing inside his boots as much as outside his boots and he wondered why he had to wear the boots anyway. It would be more direct to walk in bare feet over the cold wet ground rather than to put on these boots and then have mud in them. Perhaps his feet were warmer this way, but he was having to pick up and put down heavy boots with mud in them, over and over again. He carried his rifle by the barrel. That was wrong; he knew that. He did not need the Army to tell him that was wrong. Dan had been the best shot in Davis County and he had never carried a rifle by the barrel. What would the lieutenant say if Dan told him he had been the best shot in Davis County? He might care. Dan observed the way he was carrying the rifle with detachment and wondered about it, but he did not do anything about it. They were all moving forward in a line through tall grass and mud and that was all the Army cared about at that moment.

That morning, when it was still dark, they had come down from the big hill, and then, as the sun was coming up, across a gully. It was in the gully, in the first white light of cold day, that he had first seen the little holes in the mud and wondered about them. What sort of animal would make such little holes? They definitely were not tracks, being deeper and smaller and more sporadic than the tracks any animal, even a bird, could make. They were more like burrows, made by a very peculiar species of worm that wanted to go straight down into the ground and had the force to do it. Dan tried to picture the creature that would make such little holes. He imagined a worm with some sort of drilling apparatus on its nose. All that day, Dan spoke to no one. After the gully there had been a plain, and they had crossed that, at the same easy, sauntering pace. He could see the little holes only occasionally in the bare mud among the tufts of brown grass. He kept his mind on the worm he had imagined, the worm with the drilling apparatus on its nose, reminding himself again and again what a strange animal that would be. Then there was a short, rolling hill, with large rocks on it. Dan carried his rifle properly again. He saw something that looked like a rabbit hutch, but could not go to it, to look. They had to progress. And then there was a shallow dell, and there were many holes in the ground here. He filled in a few of the holes by scraping the sole's edge of his boot over them as he walked. Most of his walking had been easy and rhythmical, except where it was most muddy, and mostly he had kept his eyes where they were supposed to be, on the ground in front of him.

Then they were coming to a wide stand of trees and suddenly there was the noise of gunfire. Dan Prescott looked up to see where they were shooting. He saw nothing but he felt something pluck at his trousers and he looked down to see his trousers had been ripped just above his right boot. He looked at the rip and wondered how he had done that. While he was looking another hole appeared in the ground to the right of his boot. There was no worm with a drilling apparatus on its nose in sight.

Dan Prescott was standing still, looking to his left and his right to see if the line of other soldiers had left him. He could see no one. He supposed they had dropped to the ground to conceal themselves from the firing. He looked into the woods from which came the sound of gunfire and he said, "So that's what makes those holes." It was the surprise of this discovery and his eagerness to see the enemy that kept him standing.

A bulk landed beside him and something tugged at his trouser leg. The sergeant lay on the ground on his belly, his neck twisted, making faces up at him. "Get down, cherry!"

Dan Prescott lowered himself to the ground beside the sergeant but he tried to keep his head up to see what was going on. He had not thought to conceal himself. Gunfire did not frighten him.

"You know where those little holes come from?" he said.

The sergeant put his hand on the back of Dan's helmet and pushed his face into the cold mud. "You're just trying to leave your job early."

Dan lifted his face from the mud. He did not try to raise his hands to his face. He blinked the mud away from his eyes. He blew the mud off his lips. He was looking at the mud from only centimeters away.

"I never saw so many bullet holes before," he said. "All day. I thought some strange worms must have been making all those little holes."

There was a volley of gunfire. There were more holes in the mud around them.

"My father was in the big war," Dan said.

The sergeant swore. "The last war was always the big war."

The sergeant was trying to keep his head down while looking over the field. His chin scraped an arc in the mud. He spat in front of him.

Dan watched the spittle settle into the grass.

The sergeant looked at Dan with the desperate eyes of a madman. "You stay here. Don't get up until the lieutenant gets up."

"Where's he?"

The sergeant jerked his head. "Over there."

Dan looked through the brown grass but didn't see anyone. He did not raise his head enough to get his face pushed in the mud again.

The sergeant crawled away. Dan watched each hip rise and lower as the sergeant went forward. Dan likened it to the movement the worm he had imagined must make to go along the ground.

Dan followed the sergeant a few meters, then stopped. He waited on his stomach, studying the mud.

There was a long time in which nothing happened. Dan Prescott spent the time wondering what was going to happen.

Finally there was the explosion of a hand grenade from up front someplace. Gunfire stopped. Dan listened hard to the silence.

After a moment he raised his head high off the ground, even raising his shoulders in a half pushup, and looked over to where the lieutenant was.

The lieutenant was standing erect. Other soldiers were rising from the grass around him. Adjusting packs, helmets, the soldiers began sauntering forward again in a line exactly as they had before.

Dan took a last look at the holes around him, and then he got up, too, and began to go forward to the trees. A timber lane curved into the wood and after sauntering along that a few meters he found where the sniper had been. There was a gash in the ground as if something had hit it with great force. Next to it was a rifle and a human leg. Hanging from the branches of the tree above it were hunks of human meat, some with camouflage cloth adhered to them, dripping blood.

A few meters farther along the timber lane he found the sergeant flung on the ground as if hit by the same thing that had exploded on the ground. He looked as if he had been dead forever. Too, his nose and his eyes had been burned away, and that deprived him of personhood. Surprising in that cold, a fly was probing the gore of the sergeant's face.

Dan could not watch the fly too long. He turned his head and walked farther into the woods.

It was not until later that he remembered seeing the silver object sticking out of the sergeant's pocket.

2

Late in the afternoon there was a cold rain that pounded hard on Dan's shoulders. The progressing line of soldiers did not shelter from it as they had from the sniper fire.

For a while, Jack walked near Dan.

Jack was shivering as they walked and because he was shivering and they both knew it he made one big fake shiver and looked up at the sky and the rain coming down from it.

"Good day for rain," Jack said. "Cloudy."

Jack never expected a response.

"Yeah," Dan answered. "Better than mucking up a sunny day."

The rain and the mud kept going into Dan's boots and nothing seemed to come out of them. His socks were slimy. His boots slipped on the frozen ground under the mud and his feet slipped in the boots.

"Do you think the rain will make this a better world?"

"Sure," Dan responded. "Everything nasty makes this a better world."

Even after the rain stopped Jack was shivering uncontrollably so he veered away from Dan and continued walking, about ten meters away from him. The sky hung heavy over them like a cow's full udder.

Going up the last hill, Dan slipped even though leaning forward with his pack. Rifle slung, he grabbed at whatever branches and rocks he could reach. He put his hands in the mud and went up the hill on hands and feet. He reached the top on hands and knees.

At the top the lieutenant had leaned his rifle against a young tree. He was lighting a cigarette.

After sitting in the freezing mud a moment, Dan got up and went over to the lieutenant.

The lieutenant grinned as he inhaled on his cigarette.

Dan asked, "Is this where we're going to camp?"

"Camp. Yeah. We're on a camping trip. A goddamned picnic."

"The ground is frozen."

The lieutenant threw his cigarette away. "No one told you to dig in."

Dan nodded.

At the edge of the top of the hill, in the most forward position, there was a tree with its top blasted off by a shell. A meter below the burned, jagged top of the trunk were branches, one each side, looking, from where Dan stood, like outstretched arms.

Dan went to the edge of the hill near the tall tree stump and looked down at the wide, dark forest that stretched for miles below him. Wondering about the forest, and about tomorrow, he urinated as far down the hill as he could.

After leaning his rifle against the tree stump, he wrestled his wet pack off and placed that, too, against the stump. He pulled his poncho from the top of the pack and dropped it on the ground. With his back against the tree, he sat on the poncho, his legs stretched in front of him, looking up at the blasted tree, then down at the forest.

He thought of all the big guns behind him, back behind the main hill, and of all the noise they made. *If a cannon shell blasts the top off a tree in a forest, and no one is there to see it or hear it . . . has it really happened?*

Stragglers were coming up the other side of the hill. They were so muddy Dan could recognize only one of them, one who was particularly short.

The lieutenant came over with two steaming cups and handed one to Dan. "Reward," he said, "for being second up the hill. I like to know who's behind me."

In the cup was warm coffee. "Thanks."

The lieutenant was scanning the men dragging themselves into the area. "I'd love to know where my radio man is."

"Don't know about radios," Dan said.

"Look at them," the lieutenant said. "After one day. Cherry troops." In fact, the lieutenant looked reasonably clean. And from somewhere he had materialized warm coffee. "Lost only one man. These guys look like they've been out on a full tour already."

"Yeah," Dan said. "It's a great way to see the country. Nothing beats it."

"And soon the picnic truck will be here. Warm food. Today was easy."

"It's all in the planning," Dan said.

The lieutenant said, "Is this your first picnic?"

"Yes, sir. And I wouldn't have missed it for the world."

The lieutenant's eyes narrowed. "I see."

"Say, listen, sir. Are we going to see a chaplain again?"

"You want to see a chaplain?"

"Something I want to ask ... "

"There'll probably be one on the picnic wagon. There ought to be."

"Oh."

In the middle of the area, soldiers were scraping the mud off themselves, and each other.

"Not much we can do until the picnic truck arrives."

"You know the sergeant from Minnesota got his face blown off."

"He probably did."

"He did."

The lieutenant nodded down the forward side of the hill. "That's where we'll be picnicking tomorrow."

"What's down there?"

"The Kins Forest. With picnic tables among the trees."

Finishing his coffee, Dan looked at the lieutenant out of the corner of his eye.

Then he heard motors grinding and shifting. The roof of a truck cab was rocking into view over the crest of the hill. The four wheels under the truck bed were metal tracked. Behind it whined and slithered a Jeep being pushed by six men still wearing their packs.

The lieutenant snorted. "The chaplain's in the Jeep."

"What's his name?"

"I don't know." The lieutenant took Dan's empty cup. "Loomis, I think."

He went to report to the officer in the passenger seat of the truck.

Dan watched the heavyset, middle-aged man lift himself out of the passenger seat of the Jeep. Arms akimbo, the man looked around the area as if unsure why he was there.

Dan got up and went to him. "Chaplain Loomis?"

"Hello, son." The man's eyes were gray. The skin at the corners of his eyes crinkled.

"My name's Prescott. Dan Prescott."

The hand grasping Dan's was big and warm. "Where you from, son?"

"Columbia Falls, Maine."

"You want to see me?"

"I'd like to."

"Step right into my office."

The chaplain led Dan back to the tree. He leaned his back against the part of the tree that was fallen, one end propped high by its own broken branches. His eyes ran down and up Dan's body, frankly gauging the length of his legs, the width of his hips, of his shoulders.

"Quarterback," Loomis said. "Columbia Falls High."

Dan grinned. "Yes, sir."

"Team captain?"

"Yes, sir."

"What's her name?"

"Janet. Janet Twombly."

Loomis looked away. His eyes fell to the forest below them. His shoulders rounded, lowered. Absently, he said, "You look pretty fast."

"I can move it."

Loomis looked back at Dan. "How have things been going with you?"

"This counts as my first day of combat."

"So right now things are sort of jumbled. That right?"

"The sergeant got his face blown off. I was talking to him, just before. He made me get down."

"Why don't you sit down, Dan?"

Dan sat on the stump, raising his feet off the ground. "My father is a minister, you see. I was going to be a minister, I am going to be a minister, but my father said I should do something else first, get away from him, his church, Columbia Falls. He said he did not want me to be a minister because he is a minister but I should find my own reasons for being a minister. He said I should get my military training out of the way first."

"And here you are."

"Yes, sir."

Chaplain Loomis sighed.

Dan said, "Someone shot at me today. Someone I did not know and could not see shot at me. It took me time to realize that." Dan shook his head. "Worms."

The chaplain watched Dan's face a moment longer. "Will you kneel and pray with me, son?"

Dan envisioned kneeling in the mud with this man so like his father, who seemed to know him so well, and praying. "No, sir."

"All right."

Dan fingered the bullet hole in his pants. "No one who knows me would shoot at me."

"I'm sure you're right."

"Why did I come here to be shot at by someone who doesn't know me?"

"Dan, I think you've read about wars, in history class. You're here because you're a certain age, born in a certain place, at a certain time in history. The questions you ask, the questions you feel, you have to ask, and feel, because of the time, the place, your age. It was ever thus."

"What are you talking about?"

"People suffer."

"Does God suffer?"

"It is the tradition of war to kill your enemies. Doing so is called doing your duty."

"Jesus Christ."

The chaplain smiled. "That's right."

"Is that an answer?"

"Tell me, Dan, what did you expect?"

"I expected it to make sense. My life has always made sense."

"And you believed that if you did what people expected of you, you would come out all right."

"Yes."

"Because that's the way it has always been with you."

"Yes."

"Haven't you suspected that not everyone is fortunate enough to be handed a life that makes sense?"

Dan thought of Jack, and of Mary Ellen. "Yes."

"More fortunate than they, do you therefore think you should also escape their suffering?"

"I don't know what you mean."

"Dan?" The chaplain waited until Dan looked him in the face. "Do you believe your dad sent you into this?"

Dan continued to stare into the chaplain's face.

"You're all right, Dan. Listen." The chaplain grinned. "Nothing is as certain to destroy a man as a perfect father."

Dan frowned at the chaplain but could find nothing to say.

"All right, son. I guess I'm not helping much. I'll tell you what to do. Go over to the truck and get some warm food. Then get whatever sleep you can." The chaplain looked down at the forest in the dark. "You'll need your rest tomorrow."

"I thought I'd write a letter home tonight."

"Fine. Do that. Write your parents. Write that nice girl of yours. Give me your letters in the morning. I'll bring them back to base with me and see they get properly sent."

Dan let himself off the tree stump. He turned and shook hands with the chaplain. "Thank you, sir."

"Dan?" The chaplain held onto Dan's hand. "This is not my first war. I used to know what to say. I used to have answers."

"What are you saying?"

"Sorry, son."

3

His father had asked Dan to come to the church study after lunch.

It was a bright, warm June Saturday. Dan's high school graduation was only days away. He was proud and excited by his past. Without thinking much about it, he was certain his future would flow from that past as naturally, as smoothly as a turn of seasons.

He sat in one of the chairs in the study used by people who came to his father for counseling.

Sitting behind the desk, his father said, "What do you want to do, Dan?"

"What?" Everyone knew what he wanted to do. Everyone had always known. "What, sir?"

"What do you want to do?"

There was a hush to his father's voice and a seriousness in his eyes that perplexed Dan. He had never known his father to question that which was certain.

"Theology school," Dan muttered. "Become a minister. You know it."

"Do I? Do you?"

"I've never wanted anything else."

"That's what bothers me. You've never considered anything else."

"I've been accepted. You helped me apply."

"And through the entire application process, you never questioned yourself, questioned what you were doing. Sorry, son. I felt I had to raise the question."

"Do you think I'm not good enough for it?"

Behind his desk, Dan's father swung his swivel chair toward the window. He almost seemed to be talking to the lilacs in the yard. "I've been a minister twenty-two years. I've preached well, and I think I've done some good. But I find myself thinking things now I did not think when I started. I suppose I've grown in the job. All to the good."

"What are you talking about? Sir?"

"Dan, religion is not the whole truth, in that nothing can be the whole truth, for us, except perhaps the whole of human experience. And who can grasp that? The testament simply represents the truth and maybe by doing so even evades the truth, by being simple, compact, and almost comprehensible. Am I making any sense?"

"Not to me."

"I thought not." His father turned his chair to face Dan. "I guess what I'm saying is that I believe you'd have an easier time of it, and be a better minister, if that's what you ultimately decide to do, if you come into the job with less innocence, less certainty, than I had."

"I've thought about it all my life," Dan said. "There is nothing I'd rather do."

"Yes, but you've only thought about it here. The meanest thing you've ever seen is somebody throwing a punch in a football huddle. You haven't seen real life yet, felt it, and, frankly, theology school is not real life, either. You have not the experience to make such an important decision about yourself, your life. And, the world does not need another minister who quotes text without having felt the texture of existence."

"You're saying I should work a year or two before going to theology school?"

His father said quickly, "You have your military service to do, and you might be better off if you took it now and got it out of your way."

"You think I might feel differently later?"

"You'll feel differently sooner or later anyway. I believe it will be easier on you if it were sooner."

"I do want to be a minister," Dan said. "Putting off going to theology school wouldn't worry me."

"Think about it, Dan. It's a big step that not only affects you, but will affect others. This advice is hard for me to give, and hard for you to take. But you want to be sure."

Shirt off, Dan worked in the barn a couple of hours, first organizing the unused hay, then fixing a hinge a crippled cow had smashed.

Dan had not felt doubt. His father felt doubt for him. Dan was not sure if he was more shocked, or hurt.

By the time he pulled up at the pond that afternoon in the farm Jeep he was seeing his father's advice as more challenging than anything else.

Janet was in the water. Her mouth full of water, she called a greeting to him he could not understand.

He swung himself out of the Jeep and pulled off his boots and socks and jeans, leaving only his blue swimsuit on.

"Little boy blue go blow your horn," Janet called.

Grinning, Dan rushed into the water, running like a clown, raising his knees high in the air. When he dove the water swirled cold and giggling over his head and neck, down his back. He took a few fast strokes, stretching his stomach and shoulder muscles, thrusting himself forward with each stroke, kicking mightily, more for the fun of it than for any good swimming reason. The water, after the heat and the dust of the barn, felt wonderful.

He swam across the pond toward Janet. Mocking fear, she turned and swam away. He dove under her and grabbed her legs, then her waist. After threshing around in the water a moment, they were standing on the ooze at the bottom of the pond.

She splashed his face with water.

Cupping his hand before scooping the surface of the water, he sent a nearly solid wall of water into her face.

Choking, she said, "That's not fair. I can splash you, but you're not supposed to splash me!"

Grabbing her, holding her body against his, he kissed her.

"I'm drowning!"

"That's not fair," he said. "I'm kissing you, and you're supposed to kiss me."

"Wait a minute!"

As soon as the water was out of her mouth, nose, and eyes, she kissed him for a long time.

He said, "That's fair."

"I'm cold now."

"I just got here."

"Race you."

He watched her start swimming toward the bank. She held her head too high to swim well, but she looked pretty, swan-like.

Dan was sitting on the bank when she arrived.

"Beat you," she said.

"Sure."

"Well, I did. All things are relative."

"Where's your towel?"

"Over there."

He spread the towel over her shoulders and put his hand on it and moved them, gently. Even this early in the season her skin was golden. It peeked at him as the towel moved.

"I stopped at your house. Cal said you were out here."

"I was," she said simply.

"Swimming alone."

"I knew you'd come."

He caressed her long, slender neck in a nice, easy rhythm. Drops of water fell from her hair onto her neck, and glistened until he wiped them off.

"You have strong hands," she said.

"Comes from milking cows, miss."

He nuzzled the back of her neck. He kissed her, like one of the drops of water that fell from her hair, gently, and only for a moment.

Janet giggled and turned around, smiling up into his eyes.

He folded her in his arms and kissed her on the mouth.

"Nice," she said.

She put her towel on the grass and sat on it. "I had to come out early. Restless. Do you ever get restless?"

He sat beside her on the grass. "Of course."

"Now that I know I'm going to Miss Leighton's ... sometimes I just want to get going."

Janet had applied late to junior college. At first she had not been sure she wanted to leave Columbia Falls, ever.

"You're going to theology school in September," she said. "I'm going to Miss Leighton's. We might as well face it. Then you'll be the Reverend Dan and I'll be the Mrs Dan and we'll have a little parsonage somewhere. Let's go, life!"

They had never spoken formally of getting married. They just expected it. They expected their futures to flow as smoothly, as naturally from their pasts as a turn of seasons.

"That's a long way off," he said.

"Oh, not so very long. You haven't so many years of school. And they go quickly, too. Haven't the last four years gone quickly?"

"There's the service," he said cautiously.

"We can be married by then."

"Janet," Dan said. "Dad thinks I should go into the service now."

"Good heavens. What for?"

He lay back on the grass and looked at the sky.

"I don't know. I'm surprised."

"You mean, before you become a minister?"

"Yes."

"But, Dan. If you do that, you may not want to be a minister."

It took Dan a moment to adjust. "Why did you say that?"

"I don't know. It's true."

"I've never thought about it." He wondered how she had.

"Oh, hell, Dan, we're barely seventeen years old."

"What's that got to do with it?"

"Rotten wars. Rotten world. The rottenness exists out there only because people keep giving in to it, generation after generation."

"Do you think we're better off just living in this little cocoon?"

"Yes. Why not?"

"Life isn't all June Saturdays by the pond."

"I know."

"What good will I ever be to anybody if I go from the cocoon of Columbia Falls to the cocoon of theology school, and then into some country parsonage?"

"You're you, Dan. That's enough. A nice, idealistic, handsome, healthy young man. People need your strength."

"How strong will I be if I never get out of my nice warm, snuggly bed?"

"Sure. Go get yourself killed. See what use you are to people then."

"Janet."

"Men. Always make an excuse to go to war, do something violent."

"Testing the walls of existence," Dan said.

"Consciousness. Consciousness as an excuse to tempt fate, see if you get a leg blown off." She lifted his leg and put it across her stomach and rested both her hands on it. "I like your leg."

"You're talking selfishness."

"What's wrong with selfishness? Sometimes selfishness is prudent."

"I think Dad is saying I should join the human race."

Fingering the hair on his leg, she said, "You're human."

"How can I preach to the people if I haven't shared in their experience?"

"Oh, Dan."

Amazed at each other, they were silent a long moment.

Finally, he got up and held his hand out to her. "Come on. I'll buy you a cherry Coke."

She took his hand, but did not get up. "Are you going to go into the service?"

"I don't know. I think I might. I don't know. I'm going to have to think about it. Come on. I'll buy you a cherry Coke."

Graduation from high school was celebrated the next Friday.

The next month, Dan Prescott was taking his Army basic training, in Georgia.

4

Dan awoke, but he kept his eyes closed. He did not want to be awake. The heavy, early morning barrage had begun. From somewhere behind the lines would begin a roar that would go over his head, cut through the sky, then crash into the forest below him. It sounded to Dan like a railroad train rushing by, over him, then having an accident somewhere up the line. He envisioned the forest he was to walk through that day, and how the shells were breaking the trees. The bedroll was warm where he had been breathing into it. He wanted to stay as he was, breathing into the bedroll. Even though he had changed to warm, dry socks the night before, his feet were cold. He drew them up nearer the center of his body. His stomach and chest were warm because he had left his battle jacket on. His head was warm because he had breathed into the bedroll. He kept his eyes closed, saying, "Nothing is as certain to destroy a man as a perfect father."

Finally he opened his eyes and stuck his head out and looked at the world. It was gray. He saw the flash of the shells as they were fired from back where Dan had begun the long patrol yesterday. He turned his head and looked at the area around him. Except for the shells, all was quiet. It was still dark. There was no moon, but the grayness had its own light. The Jeep and truck were parked as they had been the night before. Someone was moving. He wondered who it was. Maybe it was God picking up a rifle to join in the suffering. There was someone else moving, too. He could hear someone else walking on the frozen earth behind him and he turned again but could see no one. The blasted tree stump with its outstretched branches loomed tall against the gray sky.

"Let's go," he heard.

He sat up and pushed his fist into Jack's bedroll. "Let's go."

There was a rustling from Jack's bedroll. "Jesus Christ."

Dan unrolled his pants and put them on. He grabbed his boots and forced them onto his feet. He pushed Jack again and said, "Let's go."

Dan stood up and zipped up the bedroll, kneeling on it to tie it. He tucked it under his arm, then gathered up the ground sheet, stuffing it under the same arm. "Let's go," he said to Jack.

"Goddamn it."

Dan walked quickly to the truck, tripping over the frozen ground. He was not thoroughly awake yet and he shivered in the cold. He knew he would get warm once he moved enough. No one was at the truck. There was no sign of food yet.

He threw his gear into the back of the truck. The corporal caught him by the arm. He glared at Dan through the gray light.

"Were you with the sarge when he got it?"

Dan pulled his arm away. "Yes, sir."

The corporal's face was close to Dan's. "Take anything off him?"

"No, sir. Was I supposed to?"

"No. You were not."

The corporal released the Jeep's brake, took it out of gear, and gave it a push down the slope. He jumped into it. A short way down the hill he ignited the engine.

Dan walked over to where he had relieved himself the night before to do so again. He stood at the edge of the hill, not far from the tree stump. Below him lay the Kins Forest. It stretched long and black as far as the eye could see. Shells were crashing into it on the right and on the left. It was a big forest, and if the intention was to level it before advancing by firing shells into it, it would be a long time before they got orders to march into it. Shivering with cold, Dan watched the few fires the shells had lit.

The lieutenant came to relieve himself beside Dan.

"You saw the chaplain?"

"Yes, sir."

"Don't think."

"Sir?"

"Thinking makes the true hell of war."

The lieutenant buttoned up and went away.

There was activity near the truck now. On his way to the truck, Dan tripped over something. It was soft, not like the hard earth. He prodded it with the toe of his boot. It wriggled. Someone said, "Bastard."

"Food's up."

Hands in pockets, Jack stood near the truck.

"Good morning," Dan said.

"Cheery cherry."

"Shall we take a walk today? A ramble through the woods?"

"Yeah, why not? Might bring our rifles. See if we can bag anything."

Leaning against the truck with Jack, Dan scratched his stubble of beard. There was mud in it, from yesterday.

As soon as there was the smell of food, Dan heard the lieutenant say, "Damned picnic."

Dan said, "Did I tell you my father was in the big war?"

"Yeah."

"He was," Dan said. "But as a chaplain."

"When are they going to feed us?" Jack asked.

"You hungry?"

Jack stamped his feet on the earth. "Cold. Dan, you never went to the Cabaret with me."

"No."

"So you wouldn't know which girl I'm talking about."

"I went to the Cabaret once."

"You did?"

"I was looking for you."

"Did you get any?"

"Met a girl named Mary Ellen. Talked to her for a while."

"That all?"

"She was about fourteen."

"Yeah." Jack grinned. "That whorehouse sure scraped the bottom of the barrel."

It was becoming light. There was no redness in the east and no sun yet. The gray was becoming lighter.

"It smells of snow," Dan said.

"So you wouldn't know which girl I mean."

"I only talked with Mary Ellen."

Alone, Chaplain Loomis sat on a rock across the area. Head down, he was staring into his open hands in his lap. He looked like a life study for *The Garden of Gethsemane*.

Jack said, " I wonder who's going to get into the bowls this year."

"Maybe Oklahoma."

"They're not really that good."

"Carter's pretty good. Henley."

"Henley can't run worth a damn."

"Carter's fast though."

"Michigan, for sure."

"Henley's pretty good at getting through the line."

"Yeah, but once he did, he couldn't go anywhere. He's just pure weight."

"When you're on the two it doesn't matter how much farther you go once you get through the line."

"How often are you on the two?"

"Pretty often."

"I once saw Navy," Jack said.

"Who were they playing?"

"Purdue."

"They win?"

"No. Thirteen to six."

"Why didn't they win?"

"Purdue was too good on defense. Navy couldn't break away."

"That's hell."

"Yeah. That's hell."

People were beginning to appear with food and steaming cups. Dan and Jack went to get some food. "Stick some bread in your pockets," the soldier at the back of the truck said. "We'll never see you guys again." Dan stuck a lump of bread in his pocket and grabbed his food and his coffee.

The lieutenant said, "Damned picnic."

They went back to where they had been standing, leaning their backs against the truck. There was red in the east now. Someone had slashed the cow's stomach. There was blood red all over the sky.

"Red skies in the morning, sailors take warning," Dan said.

Jack said, "Soldiers take warning."

Across the top of the hill Dan could see over the edge into the forest sprawling low and deep into the distance. The sky was red and the forest was black.

"The West Point team was pretty good last year."

"Damned good."

"Jim Blatt. What a guy." Jack gulped some of his coffee and then worked his spoon over his food, squaring his shoulders. "They should have let him turn pro, you know what I mean?"

"Yeah. I'd like to see some films of him some day."

Dan looked at the tall, burned, scarred stump of the tree standing at the edge of the hill. The two ruined branches reached up into the blood red sky. Behind and below it, low and dark, the forest stretched into the distance.

"Maybe Notre Dame will get into the bowl," Dan said. "Manelli deserves it. He's a great receiver."

"Pretty good."

"I once ran eighty-seven yards for a touchdown, on a fumble."

"You told me. That was against Gilmore High, wasn't it?"

"Yeah. They were pretty good. They had one big black guy on the team, Nelson. A real giant, a hunk of steel. He always used to hit me, hard and fast. For once I got by him."

"He used to get you all the time?"

"Hard getting a pass off with him around."

The Jeep came up the hill with the corporal in it. He tried to leave the Jeep the other side of the area but the lieutenant waved him up, leaving no doubt about it. The Jeep approached slowly. The corporal's face was red with anger.

"Joy riding?" the lieutanant asked.

The corporal got out of the Jeep. "Goddamn."

He took something silver out of his pocket and handed it to the lieutenant. Dan remembered seeing the silver thing sticking out of the pocket of the dead sergeant from Minnesota. Grinning, the lieutenant slipped it into his own pocket.

"Here comes the preacher-man," Jack said.

Chaplain Loomis walked heavily across the area, but he had his shoulders back.

"Morning, Dan," he said.

"Morning, sir."

The chaplain nodded to Jack. "Nice sunrise."

Dan looked off at the sky. Now it was turning pale yellow. Gray was closing in again.

"Smells of snow," Dan said.

The chaplain sniffed. "It does, doesn't it? Well, is there anything I can do for you?"

"I guess not, sir."

"No letter home?"

"No, sir. No letter. I never got to writing it." Dan could not have written that letter without describing the sergeant's dead face, the burned-off nose and eyes, the fly probing his flesh. "I guess I was too doggoned tired."

"What about sending a message out? I can write it down and put it in the pouch when I get back."

"No, sir. Thanks. I can write it tonight."

The chaplain turned his head away. "What about you, son?"

"Who, me?" Jack asked. Jack never expected anyone to speak to him. "No, thanks." Jack had no home to write. He was embarrassed by the question.

Looking intently at the chaplain, Dan asked, "Does God suffer?"

"People your age are quick to quarrel with the facts of existence." The chaplain put his knuckles against Dan's chin. "With age, big questions, like pimples, dry up."

Dan said, "Does God suffer?"

The chaplain shook Dan's hand. "Do your duty, son, and expect no more of yourself."

5

The truck's tailgate was slammed shut. Shells were still roaring overhead. The Jeep's engine started cold. The Jeep nosed around to head down the hill, back the way it had come. Sounding like a pig spotting food, the truck snorted around to follow the Jeep. In the passenger seat of the Jeep, Chaplain Loomis looked around for Dan, saw him, and waved. Whining in low gear, the two vehicles started down the hill. *Picnic's over.*

Dan fetched his rifle from where he had left it leaning against the tree stump. He pulled his helmet strap tight.

He looked around for Jack, but did not see him.

The corporal waved the troops forward. Clutching his rifle, Dan started down the left shoulder of the hill. He knew he was in plain sight of the enemy in the woods; to them he imagined they all looked like sticks running down out of the sky at them. Once he was within their range these people who did not know him would begin to shoot at him. Other than that, the sensation of running down the hill into the forest, helmet on his head, ungainly pack on his back, rifle in hand, his boots pounding the frozen ground, was not unlike that of running onto the football field on an autumn Saturday. There would be the rest of the team running silently. The stands would be so full they would be just a forest blur. But the stands would shift, grow taller, more colorful as the spectators stood up. And there would be cheering. He felt somewhat the same. It was colder now; the ground was harder. His boots made the same thump, thump,

thump as he ran. He was cold in the same way. He was warm on the inside because his blood ran hot, but the tips of his ears were cold, his fingers, the insides of his nostrils as he breathed in cold air. He was nervous in somewhat the same way. He was afraid something would go wrong; he would not do what was expected of him; he would appear ridiculous. But no one was cheering. There were spectators, but he could not see them.

The hill became a gradual slope and the trees grew thick. Each soldier found his own way into the forest.

There was a single shot and a single scream. A fist tightened around Dan's heart.

Dan increased his running speed. In terror, he did his best broken-field running. He pushed through brambles and bushes, ducked branches, slapped twigs out of the way of his face. His pack strap caught on a branch and Dan shouted in fear before seeing what it was that had caught him. He could hear others running, other dry leaves rattling, twigs snapping, others panting, but he did not know if this was happening behind him, in front of him, beside him. Under his helmet his hair was matted with sweat, sweat ran down his face, but his fingers were too cold and shaking to free his pack strap easily, quickly from the branch. He pounded the branch with his fist until it snapped.

The branch dangling from his pack strap, whipping the back of his legs lightly, Dan ran in a straighter line deeper into the forest. He hoped he was making up time. He heard gunfire nearby. A meter in front of him some leaves jumped. Dan fell to his stomach and rolled to his right behind a useless, leafless bush. He looked around him but saw no one, nothing moving. But he heard movement, the rush of feet and bodies through a winter wood. He crawled around the bush and forward on his elbows and knees. When he came to an open space he stood and ran straight through it.

Dan was standing in a shallow dip in the land. He felt safer than he had all morning. Finally the shelling had stopped. There was sporadic firing, but none seemed close to him. He had a clear view of each side of the dell he was in; he was certain he was alone. He would hear first and then see anyone coming at him from any direction.

Feet apart, hands on his knees, he breathed deeply, time and again, until he began to feel whoozy. He saw the stick that had caught on his pack strap, the one he had frantically broken off from the tree. It had been slapping against his leg as he ran all morning.

With hands calmer now he worked the stick free of his pack strap and threw it away.

The air in the dell was damp. The smell of snow was very sharp now. The ground was thick with dead leaves. The ones on top were dry and moved easily. Underneath, the leaves were frozen together in clumps. With his fingernails, Dan scraped centimeters of today's sweat and yesterday's mud off his face. The bushes around him were bare and cold looking. They were still but as the world settled one shoot would snap free of another and waver in the air, then be still again. The branches of the tree were bare and they mounted toward the sky without touching each other. They were graceful, making a loose, dark mesh against the cold, gray sky.

Dan lifted his jacket and took the bayonet out of its sheath. Hating it deeply, he fitted the bayonet to his rifle. To Dan, a long gun could be a beautiful thing. A long gun meant waiting in a duck blind for the world to begin again, the sun to rise, the ducks arriving quacking all their news; it meant hurrying a rabbit and then advising the rabbit with a bang it had not hurried enough; it meant surprising a grazing deer with the news it, too, was food. A long gun meant being sleepy in the warm kitchen Saturday nights, the smell of cleaning oil and baked beans, the dog at his feet redreaming the day in its sleep. With a bayonet, a long gun meant killing a man, stabbing him, slashing his stomach as high into the rib cage as one could, as Dan had learned in basic training in Georgia. For the most part, man had wished to believe himself exempt from the food chain.

When Dan heard someone running across the top of the ridge to his east, instantly he put his trigger finger through the ring. At first he could see just long legs loping. Between two trees he caught a glimpse of Jack's face. Jack's direction was neither forward nor back in the line of march, but across it. Perhaps he knew what he was doing.

Dan ran up the hill after him. At the top he waited, looking around, listening. There was a burst of gunfire down to his right.

Trying to be silent on the leaves, Dan crept slowly down to the source of the firing.

Crouched, Jack was working around rocks. Clearly his attention was focused on the center of a thick stand of brambles.

Lying down behind smaller rocks, Jack and his quarry in view, Dan got into firing position to cover Jack.

For a long moment, Jack did not move.

Then he moved. Stepping out from behind his cover, he ran toward the brambles, yelling and firing.

From the brambles came a roar Dan heard as indignant.

Jack dropped his rifle. Hit, arms flung up, his legs staggering backwards a few steps, Jack sat down, his arms trying to find his chest, his face, rolled immediately onto his stomach, rolled again onto his back, and then lay there as still as the ground.

There was no further noise or movement from the thick stand of brambles.

Dan got up and went to Jack, stood over him.

"Jack?"

Jack said, "Jesus Christ."

He was quickly dead.

Dan parted the brambles with his rifle and peered in. The corporal sat there, in one of Buddha's positions, his rifle near his crossed legs, hands in his lap. His eyes bulged beneath a bullet hole in his forehead.

Dan let the brambles swing to, close over the corporal's body.

Dan knelt beside Jack.

Jack's open eyes were hard and glazed, like any dead animal's. But there was horror in them as they appeared to stare into the winter branches of the trees over him. With two fingers, Dan closed Jack's eyes. Rivulets of blood had seeped out of Jack's mouth and nose and spilled onto his cheeks and chin. Dan took out his handkerchief and wiped some of the blood off. Despite its thickness the blood was beginning to freeze. With his hands, Dan straightened Jack's head so it was in line with the rest of his body. He tried to wipe the blood from the handkerchief onto the ground. He got off all that would come. He laid the handkerchief over Jack's face.

He got up and went down to Jack's feet and he picked up one foot, collapsing the triangle the knee had made. He put the feet together. The boots made a V. Dan tried to make the toes stay together, but he could not succeed. The heels of the boots stayed together. Jack's trousers were still tucked into the tops of his combat boots and Dan tugged at the folds of them, smoothing them out. He reached over the body and, taking the lifeless arm, bent it, placing that hand on the stomach over the other hand.

Then Dan sat back on his heels again. There was gunfire all around him in the woods, but none was too close. His own rifle was beside him on the ground. He took the lump of bread from his pocket. Sucking on the bread and then chewing it brought saliva back to his mouth.

6

Near the end of basic training in Sam's Creek, Georgia, twenty-four-hour passes were given to those who had caused no one's ire. Jack thought he'd go to the Cabaret, which was a whorehouse, so he left base without Dan.

When Dan showed up for an early dinner at the house of a local minister who knew his father, he was surprised to find two tickets for the baseball game in Atlanta that night waiting for him. An ill parishioner had given the tickets to the minister, who didn't care for baseball.

So, early in the evening, having eaten quickly, Dan found himself knocking on the alley doorway of the Cabaret. Through the doorway came the hum of voices, particularly repetitious music, and the sound of one person, a man, laughing weirdly.

Dan pounded against the door with the flat of his hand.

The door opened slowly. A skinny girl was looking out at him curiously.

"Why are you knocking?" she asked. "The door's open."

Instantly, she lowered her face.

"Hey, have you seen Jack?"

"No. What does he look like?"

"I don't know what he looks like," Dan laughed. "Just a guy."

He was looking over her head into the room beyond.

"You can come in, you know," the girl said.

"Sure."

"He might be here." She left the door open.

Dan followed her.

Inside was the smell of beer and vomit.

There were wooden tables on a wooden floor. Men, most of them soldiers, sat at the tables, mostly with beer bottles and shot glasses in front of them. Women sat across from them in the tightest skirts and sweaters Dan had ever seen. Along one wall was a wooden bar. A fat woman was behind the bar, leaning her elbow on it. She was studying the ringed fingers of her other hand on the bar. Across the room from her sat a huge man in a chair tilted against the wall. His mean eyes in a glum face darted from face to face around the room.

The skinny girl led Dan to a table near the middle of the room and sat down at it. "Do you see him?"

Dan had peered around through the smoke. "No."

"He might be in one of the rooms. You know what I mean?"

"Oh. I've got baseball tickets."

"You can sit down, you know."

"Oh. Okay."

"He might show up. You want to drink?" The girl held up two fingers and the fat woman behind the bar sighed and opened two bottles of beer.

"How does she know what we want?" Dan asked. "You just held up two fingers."

"If you come in here lookin' like you're still working on your first razor blade you only want beer," the girl said. "That's the way we figure it."

The fat woman plopped the two bottles of beer on the table and held out her hand until Dan put more than enough money into it. She was wearing carpet slippers.

"How old are you?" Dan asked.

There was a burst of crazy laughter. Empty gums showing, the glum-faced, mean-eyed man tilted against the wall lolled his head back and bellowed joyfully.

No one else in the place paid him particular attention.

"Who's that?" Dan asked.

"That's Harry," the girl said. "He laughs a lot."

Dan shrugged. "Is there anything funny?"

"Sure," the girl said. "It's all funny."

"What are you doing here?" Dan asked.

"I dunno. Same thing you are, I guess. Waiting for Jack."

"You're not even fifteen."

"What about you?" she asked. "You want to be something other than a soldier?"

"Yeah," Dan said. "A minister."

Her eyes widened. "Of God?"

"Yeah."

"Nothing wrong with that," she said. "I'm very religious. I consult my horoscope every day."

"You had to say that, didn't you."

"You know what I believe in, really?"

"What do you believe in, really?"

"I believe in Jack. I believe Jack will come."

Harry was laughing again. Head thrown back, belly shaking helplessly, he was filling the room with the sounds of mirth.

"I've got to get out of here," Dan said.

"Sure. You don't want your beer?"

"Too expensive for my tastes."

She got up and led him across the room. Her body was like a stick. Nothing moved as she walked but her toothpick legs.

Dan thought she was leading him back to the side door through which he had entered. Instead he found himself in a dark corridor with closed doors to both the right and the left.

She opened one of the doors, entered the room and pulled a chain, lighting it. In the light of the dim, swinging bulb Dan saw filthy yellow wallpaper and a single, metal framed cot in a small, windowless room.

"This isn't our best accommodation," the girl said, "but it's good enough for us."

Dan sat on the cot. "I can't believe this."

"What?" She had closed the door and was simply standing still, looking at him.

"What's your name, anyway?"

"Mary Ellen."

"Mary Ellen, you've never turned a trick in your life."

"You think I could work here and not turn tricks?"

"You must."

"Some johns like 'em skinny. Sure, a lot do."

Dan looked up at her. "Mary Ellen, you're a walking nutrition problem. Barely walking."

She sat on the bed beside him.

He put his hand on hers. "I'm a virgin," Dan said. "I want to be a minister, you see."

"I been raped."

"God."

Through the walls came another peal of Harry's laughter.

"Professionally, I sweep the floors here. Clean up."

"I see."

"I have no prestige here. And this is the only place I can go."

Dan stood up. "Won't they be needing this room?"

The harsh light of the ceiling bulb stressed the alarm on the girl's face. "God! Don't go!"

"What do you mean?"

"You're the first kid I've ever gotten into one of these rooms. Think what will happen to me if you walk out in one minute flat!"

"Mary Ellen, it's not my purpose to encourage you in this career."

"You want to be a minister, right? That means you mean to be kind, right? Walk out of here now and just think what happens to me! They won't even keep me around!"

"Good."

Mary Ellen jabbed her forefinger at the floor. "Here I get food!"

After a moment, confused, Dan sat on the cot beside her again.

"You have to get ordained, too, you know," she said.

"Not funny."

Her dress hung slack from her shoulders no matter how she pulled and tugged at it. Dan guessed she had inherited it from someone who had bought it off a rack in a poverty store years before. It was pulled in at her waist by a chipped, plastic belt in which extra holes had been made.

"This will help," she said. "They won't throw me out."

Chin in hands, Dan stared at the floor. Harry was bellowing with laughter again. The floor was filthy.

"Maybe if you swept the floors better . . . "

She smiled sadly at the dirt in the corners.

"So tell me about Jack."

"Army buddy. Somebody gave me tickets to the ball game. Thought he might like to come with me."

"You're not telling me about Jack."

"Jack. I see. Jack. He's been here."

"Tell me about the Jack you know."

"I only know what he tells me. That's the way it is in the army."

"What does he tell you?"

"He tells me that all his life he has been nothing more than a public expense." Mary Ellen tilted her head curiously. "Those are his words. Father abandoned him at birth. Mother died when he was less than a year old. About a dozen foster homes." Mary Ellen nodded. "Reform school at thirteen. Joy-riding. Again at fifteen. Shoplifting. Army at eighteen. He's full of apology for having been born."

Then, in battle, he and his corporal shot each other, by mistake.

"But is he nice?" Mary Ellen asked.

"He can't say. He doesn't know."

After a moment, Dan said, "Oh, what the hell." He began bouncing up and down on the cot. Sitting beside him, not knowing what he was doing, her head began bobbing. She turned to look at him. He shouted, "Mary Ellen! You're terrific! Oh, wow!"

Understanding, her face lit up. She began to giggle.

Sitting side by side they bounced the cot higher and higher together until the legs were leaving the floor. They made a terrific clatter. She took his hand and held it as they bounced. "Oh, wow! Wonderful!" he yelled. "Mary Ellen, you're the best!" He hoped the cot springs under the thin mattress were breaking. "Wowee!"

After minutes of this, giggling together, they stopped.

Harry was laughing insanely again in the other room.

After sitting quietly a moment, waiting for Harry's laughter to fade away, Dan stood up. He pounded on the thin walls with his fist. "Mary Ellen!" he shouted. "You're the best I've ever had!"

Grinning, he turned around to her. "At least that's true."

Eyes wet with laughter, Mary Ellen stood up. "Listen," she said. "I gotta go."

"Listen," she said. "Some day I'm going to be real pretty."

"Sure. I believe it. Older, too."

"You come back, you hear?"

1

Sitting silently over Jack's body, Dan heard snow landing on dry leaves. He looked up at the world. There were snowflakes in the air; he saw them moving quietly down the background of dark trees. One landed under the nose of his upturned face and he stuck his tongue out and licked it off. Snowflakes landed on his face, each tingling for a moment like a baby's kiss. Some landed on Jack's fingers and melted on the skin.

Someone was coming through the forest toward him.

Dan turned his head, mildly curious to see who it was, but he did not move away from where he was sitting. It was an easy matter to consider. If the person approaching was an enemy they would shoot each other and the governments would send the body bags home. Even if they were not enemies they might shoot each other, as Jack and the corporal had done. Then one government would have to send two body bags home. If the person was a friend, someone from the same platoon, wearing the same uniform, they might nod, say hello to each other, and go on together to be shot by someone else. The difference was in the uniforms. There was not much difference in the uniforms.

The lieutenant stumbled out of the woods. Blue eyes in a gray face surveyed Dan sitting cross-legged over Jack's body, the precise way Jack had been laid out.

Then he looked up at the sky. "It's snowing."

Dan said, "Jingle bells."

"Yeah. *Adeste fideles.*" The lieutenant looked down at Dan. "What're you doin'?"

"Nothin'."

"Get separated from your unit?"

"I've hardly seen anybody all day. Some picnic."

The lieutenant was a good man, Dan thought, but probably not a good lieutenant.

The lieutenant said, "Come on, soldier. Get up with your platoon."

He went into the woods without looking back.

Dan stayed where he was, sitting on the cold ground. The snow landing on the leaves was making a nice crinkling sound. Something clean and white was coming into the forest gracefully, embracing it. The snow would cover the dead leaves and the dead branches and the dead.

When Dan heard the single shot he got up and ran after the lieutenant.

A few meters into the woods the lieutenant was sprawled on the ground, his neck twisted so Dan could see the side of his face. Dan looked around but could see no one. There was not another shot. Someone had killed the lieutenant and probably run to hide further up the trail, to wait for someone else to shoot.

Dan did not take cover. He stood over the lieutenant looking for breathing, waiting for any sign of life. A small, bloodied object had torn through the back of the lieutenant's jacket.

The silver object was sticking out of the lieutenant's pocket. It was the same silver object that had been sticking out of the sergeant's pocket.

Dan stooped and took the silver thing in his hand. It was a heavy flask.

Another shot. Dan dropped the flask. Something had bitten into his leg. It was making his leg feel squeezed, instantly hot. He clutched the place with his hand. It occurred to him he had been shot; someone had shot him.

Grabbing the flask off the ground, Dan skittered for cover. After forcing himself a few meters he had to stop. For only a few seconds he leaned one hand against a tree and worked his leg up and down. Should he seek out the sniper? No, *it is the tradition of war to kill your enemies.* Yes, *it is the tradition of war to kill your enemies.* His legs had hurt many times, by being tackled, or with cramps. He had always been able to work the hurt out, by use. Now there was a bullet in his leg, or a bullet had gone through his leg. Something remarkably warm was going down his leg, inside his pants. Blood. This hurt would not work out. He was wounded.

Dan had always been able to run. Pushing off from the tree, fumbling with his rifle and the flask in his hands, hopping a few steps, dragging the wounded leg behind him, then trying to use the wounded leg as a walking stick, a punting pole, if it would not work as a leg, using it once and again to push him forward, Dan ran while he could, away from the sniper, away from the lieutenant's body, away from Jack, further and further into these senseless woods, trying to believe, trying to keep in his mind's eye sensible goal posts someplace ahead, trying to hear spectators in the stands cheering him on, loving him, admiring him, knowing he will do what is expected of him, hoping he even will do very well. But there are no dead branches on a football field and one such snagged the foot of Dan's wounded leg and Dan found himself lying twisted on the ground, looking up, seeing no goal posts, no stands filled with spectators, hearing no cheering, hearing only the hiss of the snow as it landed on dead leaves.

Then came the pain.

Using blasted, dead branches he pulled himself up. He breathed deeply, watching clouds of condensation come from his mouth. He had always been the best runner. That he could not run meant that someone had taken something very real, very important from him. Someone he did not know. He tried hobbling, but the pain was too great. He was carrying too much, the rifle, the silver flask. He took the bayonet off his rifle and hurled it into the woods. Barrel end down, he tried using his rifle as a crutch but he hated using a rifle in that way. It slipped on the frozen ground anyway. Anyway, anyway, anyway, where was he going? The snow was coming into the woods and the firing seemed far away. There was no goal.

Using the rifle as a walking stick he limped to the base of a tree, swung himself around and fell, with his back, his pack to the tree. Sitting quietly a moment he was surprised he could feel the pain from the wound in his leg in the base of his spine and between his shoulder blades and exactly at the back of his neck.

He crossed the injured leg over the other and pulled it up, bending it at the knee, so he could examine it. With his fingers he expanded the bullet hole in his trousers leg into a wide rip. Fingering the blood aside he found the slit in his skin where the bullet had entered. The bullet had gone into the calf of his leg and smashed the bone. In the same way he had torn through his trousers he expanded the slit in his skin with his fingers. He stuck his longest finger into the hole as deeply as it would go and wriggled it around, hoping to feel metal in the blood, but when he pulled his finger out again there were only small bone fragments and blood on it. He wiped his fingers on his jacket. With his boot lace and a stick he made a tourniquet for his leg above the wound, and worked it, but it did little good as the wound was a deep puncture that bubbled like a spring.

Dan unscrewed the top of the flask and sniffed the contents. Whiskey. It was filled with whiskey. The corporal and the lieutenant had had little or none of it. Why had they bothered carrying the heavy flask? Dan remembered a kid on his football team who always carried a piece of the goal post on a string around his neck. He put the flask to his lips and tried some of the whiskey. By his third swallow the pain at the back of his neck, between his shoulder blades, at the base of his spine seemed better; the blood-throbbing in his leg seemed more distant. He forced the bullet hole in his leg open again and poured some of the whiskey into it. Then he resettled himself against his pack against the tree.

Around him the world was turning white. Under his wounded leg snow was absorbing his blood like cotton.

Dan tried to think of the letter he would write home that night. He had been very good about writing home, describing all the funny things that had happened during basic training, on the various modes of transportation to the front, making a point of keeping his letters light and positive so Janet and his parents would not worry. He had not told them about his time at the Cabaret, however, about his helping Mary Ellen get "ordained" as a prostitute. His parents would not think that funny. Maybe someday he would talk with his father again about what his father had said that June Saturday in the church study, that religion *represented* truth, that nothing could be the whole truth for us except the whole of human experience. The chaplain did not know or would not say if God suffers. Dan wondered what he could write home now. He could not tell them about the sergeant's getting his face blown off just after making Dan take cover. Dan had mentioned Jack in his letters home, how Jack always won the pot at poker after telling Dan he would, but he could not tell them how Jack and the corporal had shot, killed each other by mistake simply because they were at war and had guns in their hands, a bush between them. He could not tell them about how gray the lieutenant's face was the last time he had seen him alive and the last time he had seen him. For the first time Dan's life was filled with things that were not light or funny, about which he could not be positive, he could not or would not talk.

Leaning forward he pinched the bullet hole in his leg, making blood splurt out of it. Then he stuck his thumb over the bullet hole. Blood seeped from around his thumb. He put his whole hand over it and blood seeped out from under his hand. With his other hand, Dan put the flask to his mouth and took another swallow of whiskey.

There was machine gun fire from not far away and a scream and the sound of a body threshing up leaves. Dan sighed.

He leaned his head against the tree and closed his eyes. He took a few deep breaths, pulling the cold air well into his lungs and letting it out slowly through his nose. He wondered if he could go to sleep. Without the gunfire around him, it would be peaceful here now. The whiskey had helped make him comfortable sitting against the tree. The snow hissed steadily falling on the dead leaves, falling on itself.

The third time he heard a small noise from nearby he opened his eyes.

Someone was standing a few meters away from him, with his back to him, and that someone was an enemy soldier. Dan wondered why the soldier was standing so still. Either he had not seen Dan, or had thought him dead. The soldier was carrying a rifle. He stood silently, listening, Dan supposed.

Quietly, Dan reached for his rifle and picked it up. He aimed the rifle at the soldier's back, and thought of firing. He would wait a moment. Perhaps the soldier would turn around. Keeping it reasonably aimed in his hands, Dan lowered the rifle. The soldier was young, at least as young as Dan was. His figure was light and he stood on the ground as if it were glass. He stood perfectly still, looking away from Dan, apparently listening.

They were there to shoot, kill each other. *It is the tradition of war to kill your enemies.* Dan wished they would shoot each other quickly, get it over, so they could be put in their body bags and sent home.

Softly, Dan said, "Hey."

The soldier turned around slowly. His face was muddy, too. His eyes found Dan's. He did not raise his rifle. He frowned as if deeply perplexed.

Dan raised his rifle again. He put the stock against his cheek. He found the soldier's heart in his sights.

The soldier did not move. He did not raise his rifle.

Dan was unsteady holding his rifle. His sights traveled around the

. soldier's jacket front. The whiskey had made his muscles indifferent. Also, sitting on the ground with his back against the tree, one leg straight before him, the other bent over it, gave him less than perfect control over the rifle. His finger felt the cold metal of the trigger.

Suddenly the soldier's eyes popped wide open. The skin on his cheeks tightened. He moved as if suddenly remembering where he was, what he was doing there. His left hand crossed his body to grab his rifle barrel.

Do your duty, son, and expect no more of yourself.

Dan squeezed the trigger.

The soldier's body jerked up and back as the bullet entered his chest. For some reason, his face looked astonished.

"Shit." Dan knew he had not hit precisely the soldier's heart.

Leaving his rifle behind, on two hands and one knee, dragging his leg behind him, Dan crawled over to where the soldier was lying on his back, blinking at the sky.

Again the soldier's eyes found Dan's.

"Sorry," Dan said. "I didn't want you to suffer. Guess I'm a little drunk. Also, I'm wounded, too, although not so badly."

The soldier said something in a language Dan did not understand. Nevertheless, Dan listened politely until the soldier had finished speaking.

Then Dan said, "I'll be right back."

He returned crawling from the tree with the flask of whiskey.

The soldier had raised his head enough to see Dan's damaged leg. He said something that sounded like a question.

"I don't know," Dan answered. "Same as you."

Dan sat near the head of the soldier, keeping one leg straight out in front of him, the other folded under him. He picked the soldier's head up and cradled it in his lap. He showed the soldier the flask before pouring some of the whiskey between his lips.

The soldier murmured something.

When the soldier had finished and swallowed another drink, Dan said, "The whole thing is we are worth so much and no more. If life had intrinsic meaning we would know it and surely not shoot each other, ever. The only meaning life can have is that which we create."

Dan poured some more whiskey between the soldier's lips.

Dan said, "You just heard my first sermon."

While the soldier was talking, Dan listened closely, watching his face, saying, "Yes ... yes." Dan thought the soldier looked something like the kid who used to live over the drugstore in Columbia

Falls. He had been waterboy for the football team and Dan regretted he could not remember his name. The soldier's voice became a choked whisper. Tears ran down his cheeks to his ears. He appeared to be talking faster. Dan bowed his head to listen more intently. He supposed the soldier was telling him about some things important to him, that had given his life meaning, something comparable to Dan's eighty-seven-yard run, or his girl, like Janet, whom he loved very much, or his parents. He wanted Dan to know something of himself, perhaps so Dan would realize his being a muddy-faced, weeping soldier losing his blood into the snow, his life in a battle in the Kins Forest had not been his entire reality, or even much of his life. "Yes," Dan said, "Yes . . . "

When the soldier began to cry loudly, like a child, Dan looked up at the snow falling through the winter branches of the trees. Perhaps it would help to tell this soldier about his football team. What was the waterboy's name? They had a wonderful coach. He was in his fifties but in superb physical condition. An English teacher, he would work out with the team every day. He could do anything any member of the team could do, perhaps not as fast, or as hard, but he could do it. The only way you could detect his age was by his iron-gray hair. He was tough and affectionate; he knew when to yell and when to listen . . .

The soldier was wiping the back of one hand hard against his nose and mouth. He was trying to rub away the snot and saliva from his crying but now there was much too much blood welling out of his mouth and nose to take away by any means. The soldier was choking on his own blood.

With the soldier's head in his lap, Dan gripped the soldier's shoulders in his hands and grasped them with all the force at his command, in this way, hugging him, letting him know he was not alone.

"Sorry." Dan, too, was crying like a child. "Oh, I'm sorry I did not shoot you better."

8

The snow was falling hard and steadily now. There was no wind. The ground was evenly blanketed with snow, dark trees standing up out of it against the gray sky.

Dan lifted the enemy soldier's head out of his lap and set it on the ground. Pushing himself off the ground with his hands, he stood on one leg. He tried brushing the blood off his jacket and trousers but it had frozen. He was able to stand on one leg without swaying too much.

He left the empty silver flask on the ground.

He tried the foot of his wounded leg on the ground and discovered the pain that shot up his leg to his spine through his neck was just bearable.

Limping, hopping, Dan again started through the forest, not caring about his direction, more to keep alive by movement than for any other reason. He had the thought he should be quiet so as not to wake the dead. He dragged his leg from tree to tree, leaning against each to catch his breath, plan his route the next few steps. The whiskey had made him colder rather than warmer. Mostly the pain in his leg was a sluggish throb. It felt as if his leg, spine, neck had turned into melting iron. His heart was pumping heavily, slowly. He derived some ease of his pain by keeping his jaw shut tight, keeping all the muscles in his face taut.

He wondered how he could make himself numb.

Dan came to the bank of a stream. He looked down upon it. The stream was neither broad nor deep but, in the middle, where it had not frozen, it was running fast, cold-looking and clear. It bubbled, sounding like Janet when she laughed at night in the Jeep. He would listen to her laughter through the rattle and the wind. There was vitality and mischief in that sound.

He let his rifle fall into the snow. He slipped the pack off his back and dropped that into the snow too.

Going down the bank Dan slipped. He grabbed a bush as he fell. After he landed on his hip snow still fell from the shaking bush, buttering the ground.

Placing his head upstream, he rolled onto the thin ice of the stream, rolled again toward its center, and fell through. The water was so cold at first he did not feel it. He watched the ice chips float rapidly away from him downstream. The water swirled around his neck, flowed over his shoulders, down his body, violating his clothes. Soon he felt the water moving freely on his skin as if he wore no clothes. A trail of blood from his leg followed the ice chips down the stream. Dan bit his lip against the cold. His heartbeat had increased. Soon, he hoped, he would be numb.

The stream made a path in the sky through the trees. Looking up from where he lay in the stream, Dan recognized the hill where he had spent the night before. Against the gray sky, through the falling snow the hill seemed both close and far away. He recognized the tall, blasted stump where he had sat and talked and eaten and slept the night before. From where he was now the branches stretching out either side of the tree seemed truly lifted against the sky in entreaty. The damaged tree on the hill was stark against the sky.

In frantic haste, ice breaking as he grabbed it, trying to lift his body onto it, Dan began to fight to get out of the stream. He had to get back to that hill, to that tree. However near or far it was, getting back to that position was his only way of saving himself. He grabbed a lower branch of the bush on the stream bank and pulled himself on his belly across the breaking ice, up onto the bank. He raised his good leg onto the bank and dug its heel into the snow. Using just the muscles of that leg he worked the wounded leg out of the water. Grabbing rocks and branches he pulled himself on his belly up the bank.

Again he used his hands to snake up a tree. Puffing hard, one hand against the tree, finally he was standing on one foot. He listened to the pulse in his ears. To save himself, he must get back to that tree. It did not matter how he moved; he must move. He confirmed his direction by the stream.

He tried a step or two, swinging his left leg in an arc over the inch or two of snow, and then leaping forward on his right leg, permitting pressure on his left leg for only a bearable moment. The outside of his clothes were beginning to ice. How had he ever run so fast? How had anyone ever run so fast? His right knee bent suddenly and unpredictably and threw him to the ground. He lay with his cheek in the snow, cursing himself.

It was a long way to the hill, to the tree stump, and it was becoming dark. He had to walk on the leg. Furiously he wormed his way across the snow to another tree and pulled himself up on it. On one leg he leaned his back against the tree and breathed hard.

He was looking into a grove of silver beech trees. They were slim and graceful and standing proudly apart from one another. The snow was falling straight down into the grove. There was no undergrowth here. The trees were white and the ground was white. There were several bodies in the grove. All but one were covered with snow. Dan realized that soon too that soldier would die, the heat would go out of his body, and he, too, would be covered with snow. On either side of the grove were steep inclines Dan knew he could not manage on his damaged leg. To get to the hill, to the stump, he would have to go through the grove. Through the grove and then a little to the left.

His breathing was easier. He smiled at the way he was leaning against the tree. Dan thought he had never leaned on anything in his life. He pushed himself off from the tree and stood a moment, his left foot tentatively in the snow. His knees did not buckle, and this made him happy. He took one step, trying weight on his left foot first. He swung it from the hip and placed it in the snow in front of him. Quickly he brought his right leg up with it. His bone did not break more; his knees did not buckle. He was two steps from the tree. He looked up at the sky. There was a lot of snow in it. Concentrating, he took another step, in the same, slow way, swinging his left leg first, standing it in the snow, bringing his right leg quickly up to it. He had learned how to make his legs work and he was glad. He was closer to the only body not yet covered with snow.

Then, suddenly, there was the chatter of automatic gunfire. Something gripped Dan around the waist, all at once, hitting him like pebbles but squeezing him like a hot, steel belt. He was angry because it made him lose his balance again. He lunged for a tree but no tree was there. He fell on his face in the snow.

There was no more shooting at him.

9

It was quiet in the forest. The only sound was the steady hissing of the falling snow.

Long before, the first leaves had left the trees and had fallen to be buried by other leaves. Now the first snow had come, and it was burying all the leaves together.

There had been men running among the trees in the snow, falling on their stomachs, adjusting guns, sighting along their barrels, firing. There had been bullets tearing through the poised, silent branches. Soldiers had screamed in horror and thrashed in pain. In this way, men had used, passed through the forest. Some had remained. They had sunk into the snow, shot out of their places of hiding, or chopped down as they ran from cover to cover. The snow had received them. If they were screaming, the snow hushed them; if they became feverish, the snow cooled them. There were mounds in the snow where the soldiers lay. Some were totally blanketed like rocks because they lay dead and the heat had gone out of their bodies. Some were not yet totally blanketed because they were not yet dead. The dark, shell-blasted, kneeling trees were posed like praying monks throughout the forest. There was no sound but the lisping of the snow falling through the branches of the kneeling trees and settling on the ground.

Dan Prescott liked it this way. Finally numb, he was scared no more. He thought it the finest sensation he had ever had. It was so quiet. It was like being in bed when one is so tired one enjoys the sensation of relaxation so much one does not want to go to sleep quite yet. Anxiety had left him. He heard the snow hissing as it landed around him. He did not know how long he had been that way but he could feel the weight of some snow on his shoulders. Sometimes a snowflake would land on his upturned cheek, very gently, and it would melt there, then roll off, as water. There was no snow in front of his face because his breath was warm and had made a path in the snow which he could not see but which he knew was there. He was more comfortable than he had ever been.

He had lost track of where all his limbs were. He knew they were still a part of him. A long time ago his hand had twitched, entirely by itself, and it had startled him. Perhaps it had been someone else's hand that had twitched, not his own. He was not sure where that hand was. He had the idea that his legs did not work anymore but he could not be sure because he did not know just where his legs were. They were somewhere. He really did not care.

It was in the next dawn light the medical corpsmen found him. They put him on a stretcher and carried him through the forest to an evacuation area.

By the time Dan Prescott was found, he had thought many interesting things.

10

Janet and his mother were together when his message arrived.

They had not heard from Dan for many days. Janet had been coming over every day after mail delivery to confirm that no one had had a letter from Dan. He had been very good about writing home since he had left. They were delighted now to have any message from Dan.

After reading it, together they brought the message to the church study to show it to Dan's father.

"It's not in his handwriting," Dan's mother said.

Janet said, "The return address symbols could be from a field hospital."

Dan's mother asked, "Do you suppose he could be wounded?"

Dan's father read the message:

"Compassion . . . God suffers."

JUSTICE

Claude heard the wind blowing the barnyard dust against the clapboard of the house and against the glass of his bedroom windows. He lifted his head off the pillow and listened. He could hear the barn door slamming in the wind.

The bedroom was still dark.

It was the wind making all that noise outside.

Em touched him. "Like a lion," she said.

He put his head back on the pillow and listened. Em was listening, too. They heard the wind coming down the chimney and swirling the ashes on the hearth. They both pictured the ashes rising up quickly like a tornado in a small black place, rising quickly in a straight line and then breaking out of the straight line, some falling, and the light, white bits of ash continuing to go up the chimney.

Claude thought, *coffee perhaps*.

It was a feather bed which they had had from his mother and they were deep in it. The mattress came up around any weight that was laid on it and a sheet could not be stretched taut over it but by anyone's moving in the bed would be untucked on all sides and bunched in the middle. Claude had to make a slow, pushing effort to move in it.

On the bed and coming down from their chins was the crazy quilt which had been made and left there by his mother. It had scraps of his whole history in it and the history of his family. He could have recognized pieces of the short pants he had worn when he was six years old in the quilt and pieces of his father's vest, which he almost did recognize, and various other pieces of shirts, skirts, petticoats, curtains, furniture covers and even old blankets.

"How is it going to be this year, Claudie?"

"I don't know."

Claude thought again, *I will put everything into it. I will put in the morning hours and the afternoon hours and the evening hours and April and May and June and July and August and September, one more spring and one more summer and one more early fall.*

"Perhaps we won't start," he said.

"We have enough. We have enough to start again."

"I'm not sure of that."

She said nothing.

"Look," he said. "I know what I'm talking about."

He came off that and was thinking other things, or was willing to. She said, "We have enough to start again."

So he lay silently. *What does that mean?* he asked himself. Or maybe he asked the crazy quilt or the picture of Jesus on the wall or the wind outside. *What is that supposed to mean?*

Sometimes when he spoke absolutely she would assume that he had seen something in the barn, thought something in the fields or heard something in the town that made him know this and she would keep silence and see it work out.

"You know what I'm talking about," he said.

She signed and moved in the morning bed.

He said, "We're older."

She said, "We're not that old."

"Why don't we have coffee? Is the pot on?"

"I put it on."

She had been up before he had awakened.

She lifted the quilt and, rolling on her back, she lifted her legs up and out and put her feet in the slippers on the floor.

"It's cold out here," she said. "You ought to get the coffee."

"Come back, then," he said. "I will get it."

She got into her robe quickly.

"I'll be back in a minute."

Added to the sounds of the wind Claude now heard Em in the kitchen. He heard the kitchen faucet run and the cupboards open and close, the morning talk of the cups, saucers, spoons. He heard her slippers on the floor.

He would like to be sure of it, for Emma. For himself and for Emma. They were no longer young. For the last three years he had wanted to be sure of it. Each time there had been some strange, unexpected failure of the crops. He never understood it. He understood they had no coasting money.

So it is with farms and farmers, Claude thought. *Farms fail and farmers never understand, except maybe the big agricorps owners to whom it could all be understood as calculated investment and calculated return.*

Except for the big timber companies, there were no agricorps farms around Columbia Falls, Maine. The land wasn't good enough to attract them. Claude had read of them, a long time ago, and he had never gotten over his astonishment at the idea of the big business farm, the agricorps. He had always wanted to travel south or west to really see, feel such a big business farm and to see face-to-face the man who ran it as a big business and probably sat in an office somewhere and never touched the farm as a farm. Claude wondered if the big business farmer ever touched his wife as a woman, either.

In the winter, the early winter, when he had put the whole farm in order and the lines of all were neat so that you could stand anyplace, at any angle and see all the farm lines in the twilight running neatly, proving themselves on the earth, he could feel the farm inside himself, neat, clean, nailed, raked, hinged, swung, painted, and he felt there could be no place bigger in all the world because it was bursting the bounds of his heart. It was at other times, times in the spring when the snow and rain and wind and the dripping, dripping, the bigger dripping of the land itself, moving soil away from his use, everything being wet, running, rusting, moving, giving him again a hard start, in the morning when he lay in bed hearing faint, unjustified complaints from his legs and his back, hearing Em moving with the coffee-making in the kitchen, hearing the barn door banging, pulling back on its hinges, banging *(That's not doing that any good)*, banging ... that he thought it must be nice to have a farm so big that he could go into an office and consider it on a still piece of paper rather than into the mud of the barnyard to see it as a million moving things. He felt this more every spring, in the morning, before the coffee.

He reached under his pillow and dragged out the flannel rag and blew his nose.

Em heard him from the kitchen. "I'm coming," she said.

He was comfortable in the bed. Now he could smell the coffee. He moved his head, raising his chin up on the pillow, and smelled the coffee.

He lay there a moment thinking of all the work that had to be done.

It's not the work I mind, he said to himself. He pictured himself riding the enormously expensive tractor hour after hour. At first the earth would be wet, with ice in it, and then moist and black; later, in July and August becoming lighter and drier, even dusty. He envisioned the crops always starting off well like infant children, looking just right, then growing weirdly, always something you didn't expect, dry, flooded, weak, stunted, diseased, no matter what was done for them, seemingly self-destructing. *It's not the work I mind.*

Sometimes everything went well.

Young people really do not understand in their bones all the things that can go wrong, Claude thought. *Not understanding, it is always easier to begin. Older, understanding, it's harder.*

Em came in with the coffee and waited for him to roll onto his back and sit up before putting the wooden tray on the bed. She sat down gently on the edge of the bed, half facing Claude, half facing the window that overlooked the barnyard.

The tray had been a wedding present from the Cooksons down the road. That was thirty years ago. Claude and the Cookson boy had been boyhood best friends and the wives had inherited each other. So had the children. Lucy and the Cookson girl had grown up together as best friends and had even gone to the same hospital for their training as nurses.

Neither Claude nor Em now moved on the bed, so the tray would not tip and spill the coffee.

The daylight was getting brighter, but there was no sun. The wind beat around the house.

"March comes in hard," she said. "Like a lion."

'Well, we looked at *The Old Farmer's Almanac.* It's supposed to."

Each year they memorized *The Old Farmer's Almanac* and talked about it, pointing out to each other when it was right and when it was wrong.

"Em, do you feel all right?"

"Of course I feel all right. Whatever made you ask that?"

"Oh, I don't know. Thought you'd been sort of pensive lately."

"Late winter, spring. Always gets you down. You know that."

"I know."

"I always feel better when I see things turning green."

She poured them each more coffee. He had a great big cup, white with a big handle on it for his big finger. Her cup was smaller and of bone china. She drank tea from it every afternoon.

"I thought you might like to get away from the farm. You know."

"Now, how can we possibly do that? It's almost plantin' time."

"You know what I mean. Sell out. Live in the city."

"And who'd feed us?"

"I can work in the city as well as here."

"Doing what?"

"Well, I've been thinking. It would seem to me there's always need for a good carpenter."

"You don't belong to a union. And you know what Doc Lambert says about unions."

"You listen to Lambert too much. Him and his talk about cities. Never heard a man talk so much about hatin' cities."

"Well, he went to a city medical college. And, besides that, he lived in the South, too."

"When."

"When he was a little boy."

"I know that."

"A lot of folks don't like cities, Claudie. They're not made for us."

"Oh, I don't know. Wouldn't you like the movies and the department stores and maybe go to a real restaurant sometimes?"

"Columbia Falls is fine enough. Plenty right here we never use. Plenty of nice people right here we've never even met."

"Who?"

"The Brices."

"I've met them."

They had met the Brices once. And Claude and Em had talked about what nice people they were. The Brices had retired to Columbia Falls from Michigan for some reason and met the town at the Congregational Church. Reverend Prescott had introduced them to everybody.

Mrs. Brice had thrown herself into the community with a good heart, but her efforts had not come off too well. She had introduced the Girl Scout cookie to Columbia Falls. She had not understood the people of rural Maine did not like to sell small things to each other, ask each other for small favors. When the people needed each other they needed each other in a big way, and needed to be able to approach each other without many small indebtednesses between them.

Everyone liked the Brices, but few had gotten to know them.

"I could work in the cement works," Claude said. "Lucy's husband could introduce me."

"You're fifty. There are plenty of youngsters lining up for those jobs. And what would you want to work in a noisy factory full of dust for anyway? You'd go crazy."

"I'll tell you why. I'd draw a weekly paycheck, that's why."

"Well, we're not starving."

"Look, we've had three years of bad crops. And there's nothing saying we won't have a fourth bad year."

"It's time we had a good year."

"It was time last year."

"And anyway, even if it does fail, there's always the government."

"I don't want to file again."

"Why not? We paid our taxes, when we had it."

"I've just never figured the government for a partner."

"Bosh. You're being silly, Claudie."

"Now don't tell me I'm being silly." Claude drank some of his coffee. More quietly, he said, "It's the starting over every year that gets me. Always having to begin again. How come at age fifty I have to start again?"

"That's the way it is," Em said. "If you don't keep startin', you're finished."

In their silence then for a moment Em was filled with the idea it would be the greatest year ever. The idea even came into Claude's head for a moment. The soil would stay brown and rich and the harvest would be full. It would be such a great year that he could even get that enormously expensive tractor finally paid off and put down for a new truck and maybe she could get a new winter coat, and shoes.

It was only for a moment that they had this idea. The house was close to the barn and the wind was beating them both, banging the door of the barn and hitting the house with leaves and twigs. They heard the horse kicking the sides of its stall.

"Well." Em was looking out the window into the barnyard. "We have enough to start."

MEWLING AND PUKING

Listen from the womb, O big man world.
Hear you the sound of wind in the trees?
Some cave, some womb, some swaddling cloth.
Hear the sound of wind in trees.
The place is warm and snug.
Hear the sound of the wind.
A hearth with fire burns.
Hear sounds of the wind.
Rain on the roof.
Hear sounds of rain.
Wind, rain, warmth.
Hear the wind.
The womb.
Hear wind.
Doom.
Hear.

The doom, the doom, the doom, the doom:
You hear, you feel, you see, the doom;
You see, you feel, you hear, the womb:
Always, always, always, the womb.
The womb, the womb, the womb, the womb.
Gather in: your feet, your hands, your arms, your legs.
Gather in; yes, gather in, and gather in,
And gather, in some womb, the doom, the doom.

*   *   *

All this tender world, the soft,
The safe, unbreathing state:
Oh, be thus deep,
Feel this comfort;
Stretch and turn,
And gather in,
Gather in,
Gather in,
And gather in the
Womb: doom, doom, doom, doom.

Awake, then, Wonder. Awake.

The fog. The gray. The warm. The moist.
Fog. The sifting. Floating. Rising.
Fog.

Puffs softly by the body creep,
A floating in suspended air,
Push naught against the body now:
The puffs and clouds and swirls of fog;
A flame of something far beyond.
Oh, gather in, the flame, the fog.
Something drifts from the fog to fog,
And over fog, to fog beyond,
To fog again, again to fog.
And there is this space, now filled with
Present, dodging, receding fog;
There, there is earth, now weighing fog,
Sweated with the work of weighing weight.
There, there see some sputtering flame
Visible in the lift of fog.
A hollow laugh, far beyond fog.
Reach way up in the hill of fog
As fog goes by.
There is the sound from far away
Of horses' hooves on cobblestones,
A neigh: silence, but dimly heard.
The noise of Wonder is ashriek:
Who could be there? Who would touch me? Speak!
Soft fingers of a somber fog . . .

Is this a room within a house,
Street within a well-walled city,
Some mountain cave below a cliff,
Some narrow corner of the womb?
A flame, of something, far beyond . . .

Let the bells ring on that bring us forward,
Away from womb to fog to snow to light;
Let them peal from every knoll and tower,
Tolling, knelling in dampen'd atmosphere.
The sharp but somber singing of the chimes
Roll on before us in the hiding fog
And ring beyond the never telling snow.
And women from their casement windows look,
And call to men in yards below, to see.
And children dance and shriek a festive air;
Dogs, cats and mice perform strange fantasies.
But, Oh, the counterpoint of sadness here!
Move on, the lamppost whispers, on and on.
This gleam of light is not enough, but on
To beams of brilliance.
          Oh, give me brothers!
that they may march along with me!
          My brothers
March in proud parade, some before, behind.
And in their dark and praying faces shines
Again the light, containing it, all years
There be within the cupping of a cowl.
And on and on we march, stepping
To the stately rhythms of pealing bells.
Fog drifts from man behind to man again.
The white becomes a gray and then a blue;
Stop: all the world beside the stream is still.
See: the white-robed maiden in the snow.
And in this maiden's hand there is this stand
Of seven lighted candles, blackened sticks.
Now Wonder watched and saw the first man stare;
A single light went out. The second sprang
To save his light; another flame went out.
A third man knelt in prayer; lost his light.
So the flames extinguished in Wonder's sight:
The fourth man did some strange and holy dance;

The fifth man warmed himself and cooked his food;
The sixth man drew his sword and offered fight.
And Wonder cried in small boy's woe, afraid
For him there'd be no light with no flame stayed.
Suddenly, then, the fog and snow withdrew
And left the earth in brown, gold, verdancy.
The maiden handed him the only light,
And ordered him: Be;
Take, for you to see.

Air is not for us to know just now;
It is a mystery. Pull it from one place
And it is there again. No: it is contained.
Continue to pull it,
To push it,
To grab it,
To hold it,
To cup it,
It is not here nor there nor anywhere seen;
It is here and there and everywhere: it is contained.
Gather it from the trees and press it to the ground.
Where is it? It is contained.
Suck it in your cheek and it is gone, yet
It is there: it is contained.
So are the mysteries well founded.

Flame is not for us to know just now;
It is a mystery. Only by its own light
Can it be seen; by its own existence,
It exists,
So writhing,
So twisting,
So wriggling,
So dancing.
It is not still or moving but always placed;
It is still and moving and always free: it is contained.
Gather it from the wick and press it to the ground.
It is not there. It is contained.
So are the mysteries well founded.

It is not for us to know just now;
It is a mystery. Clean and brackish, it

Covers and conceals, makes lost and obvious,
Is to itself but true.
Sea water,
Pond water,
Plant water,
Man water,
It comes from here, goes there, and is back again;
It is here and there and everywhere: it is contained.
Throw it in the air and it is gone, yet
It is there: it is contained.
So are the mysteries well founded.

Earth is not for us to know just now;
It is a mystery. Surely it is there,
Comes snow, is no longer there, yet underneath
The snow, the sea, and me,
The hard earth,
The dry earth,
The soft earth,
The damp earth;
Splash it into forest pond, it is not there, it is;
Move it, there is more, move it, there is more: contained.
Gather up the soil, where to hide it, where? where?
Where to put it where it isn't? Contained, contained.
Hide it in the seas, to mountains run: contained.
So are the mysteries well founded.

In the midst of springtime valley
Stands a newly powered Wonder
Hearing the earth in crack and sigh
As life seeps through to morning air.
The wisp of freshness hits his brow;
The bursting green and brown and blue
Fills Wonder's sense with thrill and fear.
Walls of distant snow-capped mountains
Now make his crib; untouchable
Clouds remind him of early fog.
He sees the upward pushing greens
By silver, tinkling, whip-backed streams;
Drying earth seeps in harmony:
Sun, wind, earth and water chords are struck.
But, Oh, the terror of the earth!

Oh, the emptiness of plenty!
Wonder sees, knows only the birth
Of all these things, knows not of them,
Composed, disposed . . .
Is this again deceptive state,
Watery lines and wispy lights,
Or are the mountains always there?

He looks about, sees his shadow
Alone; no other shadow's there;
Looks: cannot find another self;
Sees reflections in the water
Of trees, and rocks, and other things;
Stoops to see himself, but cannot.
Below the water surface swims
Another self? an aimless fish.
It is not he!
It has to be.

He runs to nearest tree, climbs up
To a hidden spot of safety
Among the leaves and
Himself reflects.

So are the mysteries well founded, amen, amen:
So terse, so sharp for truth,
So cutting, so defined,
So true—untrue to form;
So, self-doubting, Wonder speaks,
So self-blaming and defiled,
So conscious of an empty stomach,
So eager to go, to go.
So. So. So.

The nymph stood within the forest
Edge, and coming down to meet him she left
The forest darker by her descent. "Come,"
Said the little nymph, "you are most chaste and
Still to see the things that be, so come." And
Taking Wonder by the hand she entered,
And stepping soft among the stones, treading

Light on leaves, she peered around till Wonder
Tugged against her hand and discovered not
The question he would speak. Through the forest
Glades trod they, aimless through the leafy trees,
Aimless playing with the bees, aimless
Lolling on the shady grass, aimless bathing
In strange-colored streams, ever on, through the
Valley floor and up a little, sunlit
Slope, and, looking down, Wonder saw a cave . . .

"I'll not be contained," pled he, "not contained!"
The nymph sprang back, freeing their fingered tie,
And looking at the boyish Wonder, said,
Most fiercely, "Why, no, you are not chaste!"
And off the nymph sprang lightly, and chasing
After her, the forest glades grew cold and
Colorless, an unknowing yet badly
Punished Wonder ran and tripped and at each
Step he knew he fell behind and wind sprang
Up and Wonder believed he saw the nymph
Atop a mountain, and climbing up in
Chase, the wind beat against him; and sylphs,
Too-righteous prudes, chanted most tearfully,
"You are not chaste! Chase! Chase! You are not chaste!"
And so chanting they ran around, around
The mountain peak. And Wonder, crying, struck
At them, and down the mountain side ran he.
And in the valley, the gnomes leapt around,
And, clapping hands, they screamed into his ears:
"Chase! Chase! You unchaste thing! Tell us all that
You'll not be contained!" And on ran Wonder
Through the rock-strewn plain and over windy
Heath with laughing gnomes and chanting sylphs and
Far ahead, perhaps the nymph; and from a
Pool from which rose a stink, up there clambered
Salamanders and, striking Wonder, they
Dragged him to the boiling water to burn,
To baptize, and to bathe. Through dark, hot,
Leaden air, this unchaste Wonder was
Flung. Falling, falling, falling he landed.
Sinking, sinking, sinking, Wonder was no

More, he thought, and then again, he was. And
Coming out, he no longer looked for nymph,
Nor were there gnomes, nor sylphs, nor salamanders.

And coming out, he no longer looked for nymph,
No, nor gnomes, nor sylphs, nor salamanders.
And coming out, he saw the night was deep
And heard the lions roar from their distant,
Hidden dens. So standing, hungry, wet, cold,
He felt the mountains, rivers, the forests,
Fog within him, standing poised in strange,
New scenes.
      And taking his lonely candle,
He touched it to a pile of sunbaked things:
Flame echoing flame.

SANS EVERY THING

1

The house was near the center of town on the main street. It was a white house with curtains in the windows and a black, slanting roof. Green bushes ran around it. A white picket fence ran between a small lawn and the sidewalk.

In the summer Doc John would go out onto the front porch in the mornings and sit in his rocker. He said the rocker was good for his back. He usually had a copy of *The Reader's Digest* and *The Columbia Falls Journal* in his lap which he would leave there all day. One day he had brought out *Tales of a Wayside Inn* which he had looked into and found he had forgotten how to read and had left in his lap all that day. When the postman came up the steps and saw the book he made some comment, which pleased the old man. When the postman was going away the old man picked up the book and opened it and looked at the pages in case the postman should look back. He had given up reading.

The previous summer he had been able to walk down the main street with his cane to the drugstore in the afternoon and drink a strawberry ice cream soda with the ice cream perched on the rim of the glass. But the boy kept forgetting to perch the ice cream on the rim of the glass so Doc lost interest in going down to the drugstore. This summer he did not walk at all. He stayed in his rocker on the porch and watched the other people go by, walking along the sidewalk the other side of the picket fence.

In a bedroom inside the house there was the old man's daughter, Holly. She was very sick, and she knew how sick. She had Miss

Slade, the town nurse, all the time. But Holly felt certain she was not going to die. The old man had been dying all these years and she would continue to take care of him the same way she had taken care of her husband when he was dying. She would take care of her son, Steve, too, and help him not go to the city. That was the way Steve was inclining now. The town was too small for him. Holly was certain she would live to make Steve see going to the city was wrong for him, there was nothing there for him, that Columbia Falls was a nice town, and that she and Doc needed him. She had tried to get Doc to say something to the boy about his future. They had always liked each other. Steve was good with the old man. But the old man was getting worse every day. In bed in the small house, hoping she would not die, Holly could hear Doc rocking back and forth on the porch in front of the house.

In the beginning there were the flies, the old man thought, and they were not good. Even in the morning in the beginning there were the flies. They were never any good. They think they can play with my ears, even inside them. Wonder what Holly would say if I told her the flies play inside my ears? She would say, "You've got bugs in your head, all right. You're buggy."

That Holly. She was never afraid with me. Hell, she was never afraid of anything, really afraid. She was always pulling to go out on calls with me, no matter where, no matter when, no matter what the call was. "Dad, will you take me with you? Just this one call?"

That time she went out with me to McKensie's farm and Holly saw the blood all over the kitchen floor from where the baby had vomited itself to death. I'll never get over the way Holly held tight onto my sleeve and watched me wash the baby off in the kitchen sink and wrap it in McKensie's red sweater, which I found on a peg in the back hall, and put the wrapped baby in the packing box McKensie had brought from his cellar. The baby's mother, McKensie's wife, was in the kitchen screaming and McKensie tried to keep his arms around her and she kept fighting him off. Holly wasn't afraid. She was just eight years old but she wasn't afraid. She just held onto my coat with her little fist and came outside with me and held the light while I dug the hole.

The ground was hard, it being late in October. There already had been one frost. Doc put the box down at the door of the shed and felt around inside until he found a shovel. Holly stood outside with the light, standing over the box. They could still hear the McKensie woman screaming in the house. With the shovel under one arm and the box with the baby inside in his hands and with Holly tagging along behind holding onto the skirt of his coat he went down to the meadow behind the barn and dug the hole in the hard ground, digging up stones and roots and rocks or soil encrusted with ice. As he dug deeper the soil became softer. He put the box in the ground and shoveled dirt on top of it. McKensie had asked him to do this. He said it was bad enough having their baby born with a weakness which soon killed it without having to accept the ordeal of the town's sympathy at a public funeral and burial. They just wanted the baby buried somewhere on the farm. Doc tried to conceal the place he had buried the baby so the McKensies would not have a place on their farm they would not look at or step. But when he got done there was a mound of fresh soil behind the barn and there was not much he could do about it except stamp it down and scuff leaves and twigs over it.

No, sir. I never did understand why babies die. Still don't. Can't tell me life has intrinsic meaning when creatures are born into it who don't have a chance. When a baby is born with a weakness that soon kills it, is the meaning of its existence supposed to accrue to itself, or to its parents? The death of a baby has always struck me as just useless grief.

Well, then again, I suspect there were babies that were planned, at least hoped for, that never were conceived.

Steve is my boy, removed one generation, of course. Holly's son. She had him off that Fred What-was-his-name, my son-in-law. She worked in the bank until she was forty, married Fred Jack-a-knapes, then had her first and only child. She tended the baby while helping Fred die of world-weariness. Worked two rooms at once, for a while there, a bornin' room and a dyin' room. After a while, she returned to work in the bank. Some life. At least we got Steve out of it.

I think Steve likes me, but he pities me all the same. A man does not need to be pitied by a boy. He thinks I'm old and deaf. Of course he's right about all that. I'm no spring chicken. And I do not hear correctly everything that is said to me. Maybe he will take a walk with me after supper tonight, if I don't fall asleep. I'll show him I can walk as far as the drugstore, anyway. I'll buy him a strawberry ice cream soda. Maybe Holly will slip me the money on the quiet so I can surprise him with it and buy him a strawberry ice cream soda. The boy will be along anyway. He will come. In case I get tired, he can encourage me home. That's the thing about children, your own children. Mostly I find them encouragin'.

I could have had more children than just Holly. I planned on it.

Youth, though: youth is a wonderful expectation. That's why youth can afford to be so encouragin'.

In the morning Johnny looked out his open bedroom window to the meadows. He was thirteen years old. There was the yellow field with the sunlight in it and the brown fence around it and dandelions growing around outside. Francesca stood over by the fence trying to put her mouth out between the rails without getting her horns stuck. She was reaching for the dandelions that grew outside the pasture. She had eaten all the dandelions that had grown inside the pasture. Beyond the meadow with the sun in it there was the bank of pine trees going up the hill steeply so that it appeared a tall wall with irregular brown chunks in it where the wood itself and the earth of the hill could be seen.

Johnny breathed deeply two or three times, smiling, and then went to the mirror and showed himself his muscles. He lay down on his back on the floor, his head under the foot of the bed. Gripping the foot of the bedstead in his hands he lifted the bottom of the bed as high over his head as he could reach, up and down twenty times. Then he showed himself his muscles in his mirror again, still smiling.

Of course youth doesn't know what to expect; it just expects.

What did I expect?

Surely not my trinity of women. Surely not platonic exhilaration, efficient, loving frigidity, and the kind of passion that led to murder and betrayal.

Steve came out of the house to the porch where the old man was sitting. He was munching a piece of toast.

"Good morning, Steve."

"Mornin', old fart."

"How'd you sleep, boy?"

"Couldn't keep count of my wet dreams, I had so many."

"That's good. Going to play ball?"

"Going to take that redhead on Cherry Brook Lane up to the pond and pound her bones for her."

"That's good. How's the team doin' this summer?"

"Triple play, Doc. Got three pregnant already."

"Well, that's not bad. Keep hittin' them in there, boy, keep hittin' them in."

"I will, Doc. Jeez, why doesn't somebody wipe that drool off your face? It's disgusting!"

"That's right. That's perfectly right. Say, did I ever tell you about the time your mother came with me, up to McKensie's place?"

"And the blood and guts and crud were all over the kitchen floor and the wife was swingin' at the husband and you wrapped the dead brat in a sweater and put the whole mess in a box and buried the box behind the barn? No, you never told me that. Only a thousand times you never told me that."

"I guess I did tell you that one."

"Did I ever tell you how tired I am of you and your same god-damned stories and your same goddamned questions about the non-existent baseball team every morning? How goddamned tired I am of this goddamned town? Have I ever told you all that?"

"That's right, son. It was McKensie's red sweater. The things a town doc used to find himself doin' in the old days . . . "

"Goddamn McKensie's red sweater. It's rotted in the ground with the goddamned baby years ago. As you should have, you god-damned old fart."

"She was very brave. Your mother was always very brave, Steve."

"She's in there dying, goddamn it! And you're out here rockin' away, gaga and grinnin', pretending to read, remembering things from last century that not one goddamned person cares one god-damned thing about!"

The Reader's Digest slipped off the old man's lap.

Steve bent over and picked it up and put it back on his grandfather's lap as if the gesture, the movement meant nothing to him, it was so easy for him, as if he did not even know he was doing it. For a moment, the boy's hand remained on the hand of the old man, and pressed, gently.

Doc looked into his grandson's eyes and saw worry, and sorrow, and fear.

"She'll be all right, Steve."

The boy put his hands in the back pockets of his jeans.

"Look, Steve! A fly! Have I ever shown you how to kill a fly?"

"Only a trillion times."

Steve watched his grandfather slap his hands together an inch or so over where the fly rested on *The Reader's Digest*. When the old man's hands separated, the fly dropped out of them, dead.

"Works every time!" Doc chortled. "Never fails! Not once in a million years."

"You should know." Hands in his back pockets, Steve went down the porch's steps to the street.

"Play good," the old man called after him. "Play good."

2

In conclusion, it's my considered opinion that people who are cheated one way or another cheat others and sometimes themselves.

Sometimes it's a good thing; sometimes not.

And that's about all I know about life.

Sometimes I must admit I'm tired. Especially of the problem of communicating. I do wish it were easier talking to Steve these days. I'd know more of what's going on. I'm sure he tells me. I have to pretend, cheat a little. I have to steer the conversation, hoping he says the obvious things to what I say. When I don't know what he said, I have to change the conversation. You learn certain tricks when you're a little hard of hearing. Even with tricks, you miss some of the details. I can't be tired now, though. It's only ten o'clock in the morning. I wonder what time it really is. The postman hasn't come yet. I guess I have the tiredness that just comes from being alive.

Music is a fine way of communicating, sir, a very fine way indeed. I can't hear the music much any more, though. I can't even hear the loud music they have on the radio. I mean I can hear it; I just can't make it out. You can hear the noise; it just doesn't make much sense. Funny the way young people speak so softly but like their music so loud. The music makes them twitch. It's fun to watch Steve. When the radio is playing its loud music his knees bounce even when he's sittin' down. His fingers twitch, his elbows jerk, his whole body just shakes up and down, all the while this steady look comes into his eyes as if he were as still as a rock. He looks like he's about to take a spasm. Then his lips move when he speaks to me and I can't hear a thing. I wish I could hear the music.

Well, I heard music. I heard music no one else in the world heard. I had nearly forty years of private concerts by an artist almost anytime I wanted them, which was frequently.

I say Amy was a concert artist. I know almost nothin' about music. But there's no one alive to say I'm wrong, and there never was.

Amy was a girl of sixteen when Johnny and his mother moved back to Columbia Falls. Johnny was younger than Amy by three years. They were distant cousins. She had a clear face and wide eyes and a pigtail braided down her back. That was how he was always to think of her.

The story was that she had had her foot crushed by a hay wagon. The old doctor in Columbia Falls thought he set all the bones in the foot correctly but bones in the foot are very difficult to set. When gangrene set in, he took Amy's foot off to save her life. That first fall she struggled on her crutches the three miles to school and home again most days, but once the snow came she no longer could make the trip. In the spring she never showed up at school and everyone pretty well forgot about her.

In the spring of Johnny's thirteenth year he spent a lot of time wandering over the hills of Columbia Falls trying to get used to it, practicing by himself how to talk in the flat way the people around there talked. Johnny had a southern accent in those days which amused the other children but which they found just too odd to use in real conversation, real relationships.

One afternoon, wandering, he came to a hollow in the fields and lay down on the thick, dead grass. The woods had not yet come into bloom and the ground was still cold. After lying there a while, trying to say *damn* to himself, quickly and sharply like a Northerner, with only one syllable, he heard a piano playing. He poked his head up over the edge of the hollow and saw a house on top of the hill. He had never noticed it before. Johnny lay on the cold grass tufts and listened to the piano that afternoon until it finally fell silent. He did not understand about music, that usually it was something written, then read, learned, interpreted and played. He apprehended it as sound. And here this musical instrument in a big old house surrounded by nothing but fields and woods was making this wonderful sound that did everything to him, made the hair on the back of his neck prickle, made him smile, frown, doze. In the dusk he waited for the piano to start again before finally giving up and making his way home.

He asked his mother about the house on the hill and on Sunday afternoon he and his mother went to visit their cousins who lived there. Before that his mother had referred to them only as Ethel and her husband and their daughter who was a cripple.

Tea and cake were passed around the small front parlor. An upright piano was against an inside wall. Johnny waited for someone to play for them, but the topic of the piano never came up. Each time he looked at Amy she looked away.

After an hour or so, Amy got up from her chair and put herself on her crutches and took herself out of the room.

Johnny followed her into the kitchen.

Perhaps speaking too flatly, too definitely in his new accent, in his new masculinity, he said, "You play the piano."

"No," she said. "I don't."

"Does your mother, then?"

"No."

"Your father?"

"No one here plays the piano."

"I've heard you," Johnny said.

"Oh, no! No, you haven't heard me!" Amy's face wrinkled, near tears. "Please don't say that!"

"But I have."

"Please don't say you ever heard it!" Standing on her crutches in the kitchen, Amy brought the heels of her hands to her eyes. She sobbed. "Please, please don't ever listen."

"Why? Why not? I surely did enjoy hearin' you play. I appreciated it."

"Please! I couldn't stand it . . . the thought of you out there somewhere in the woods listenin'!" Almost falling off her crutches, she reached out her hand and pushed Johnny flat against the cellar door. "You leave me alone! I hate the funny way you talk! You go home, Johnny Lambert, and don't you ever come back!"

Amy swung her way out of the kitchen on her crutches, stopping in the hall to work her fingers over her eyes and face. Johnny followed, trying to go slowly enough so she would stay ahead of him. He did not think it polite of him to catch up to her when obviously she was trying to hurry. The two sat in the parlor not talking for the rest of the visit. They did not look at each other. Johnny felt as if he had broken a bowl of china or some other precious thing in that house.

Over many years, John went to listen to Amy play, many, many times. During some periods of his life he attended her concerts as many as two and three times a week. He would wait hidden outside her house to hear if she would play and was glad to listen when she did, sad to miss her playing when she didn't. But he never did say he heard her. He never went to the house again. When he saw her in the town, which was seldom, he never spoke. During his high school years, later when he was home from medical college, still later when he was a doctor making his rounds, he would go to two or three hidden places he had discovered around the house, first to the hollow, then to a stand of pine trees the other side of the house, later in his buggy, still later in his car to an old wood lane that ran behind the house and he would listen to Amy play the upright piano he never saw again. He would listen to her music in the clear spring air, together with the crickets in the summer, blowing on autumn winds, muffled in the winter snow. He began to forget what she looked like. As she became older, Amy became a complete recluse. Never having learned to read or write music, John figured she was composing as she went along, pouring this enormous energy, her life into something that had no meaning to anyone but herself, and, unbeknownst, to him. John guessed this music created some sort of an illusion of life to Amy, an illusion that would be shattered if people knew of her playing the piano when she never had been taught to play. Most likely, he realized, she did not play well, according to the standards of everyone but her, and him. He came to identify different themes as she played them, heard them evolve and be treated this way and that, sadly, happily, then slowly fade out of her repertory, replaced by some new theme. Her playing was never just one thing or another, never just happy nor sad, violent, tumbling nor gentle, soft; it was everything within one session, one concert: expressing all the feelings and ideas that can exist within one person at one time.

When Amy was fifty-four and Doc John fifty-one he heard of her sudden death and went to her funeral on that Tuesday morning. No one in the community except himself and her very old mother knew Amy had devoted her life to making sounds from the piano. Few attended.

On the church organ *Resurrection* was played, which is a very usual thing to play at a funeral.

The human machine is the only machine on earth that sometimes works better when it is a little bit broken. By our aberrations do we make meaning. Think what we would have lost if Mozart and Bach, Caesar and Napoleon, Van Gogh and Picasso had been sent to head doctors and turned into normal people. Would it have been possible? Doctors can do anything these days. Like hell we can. As we used to sing in medical school, When in doubt, amputate. I've never seen normalcy as a desirable social goal. I escaped it, I'm glad to report. Of course I wasn't far from normal. I just had a different regard for the use of my hands and for things that live and breathe. Half an orphan, I was on my way to being a mama's boy. That was my only abnormality. That goddamned woman. Mrs Corbet was her name. She fretted me, made me discover my abnormality, and still I call her a goddamned woman. What if Dante and Shakespeare and Milton had been made to sit down three times a week and tell their illusions to a head doctor? There'd be no wildness, no poetry in life if people weren't a little bit broken. History would be a blank. I'm sure people regretted Amy's life, if they knew of it, or cared. I suppose it selfish of me, but I appreciated her. That was the way it had to be, for her. Maybe, just maybe she was happier, more fulfilled with a missing foot than all the people I've known who've used their feet just to kick up a fuss. Certainly Amy was unique.

When Johnny was fifteen he was sitting on a stone wall near the center of town one day, knitting.

Mrs Corbet was out walking her two dogs. When the dogs saw Johnny on the wall they jumped on him. Leaving his knitting in his lap, he petted them with both hands.

"Why, Johnny, what is that you have there?"

"Hello, Mrs Corbet. My knitting."

"Your *knitting*!?! What's the matter with you, boy?"

"I'm fine, ma'am."

"Does your father know you knit?"

"My father's dead, ma'am."

"Your mother should be ashamed of herself!" declared Mrs Corbet.

"She had nothing to do with it. He died at work."

"Letting a boy knit! Did she teach you?"

"Oh. Yes, ma'am. She says it's good for my manual desterity."

"It's sissy! What kind of a man will you be when you grow up?"

"We're making a sweater together, my mother and I. I'm doing the sleeves. I'm really pretty good at it. See?"

He held up the half-made sleeve for her to see.

"And the word is dexterity. Do you lisp as well?" She stuck her tongue between her teeth and wrinkled her nose at him, ugly.

One of Mrs Corbet's dogs seized the knitting in its mouth and ran up the sidewalk with it. The ball of yarn was pulled out of Johnny's lap and began unraveling on the sidewalk. Johnny jumped off the wall. "Here, you! Stop that!"

The dog was shredding the half-made sleeve.

"Don't yell at the dog, Johnny! It's doing what it knows is right—taking the knitting away from a half-grown boy! I'm glad someone has the sense to!"

Without another word, Mrs Corbet followed her dogs up the sidewalk.

Fuming, Johnny kicked what was left of the ball of yarn at his feet.

Johnny went home and made a rabbit trap from an advertisement he had seen in a magazine. The advertisement described how good rabbit stew is and how rabbit skins can be sold to make fur coats and the rabbit feet as good luck charms.

Finished, he set the trap in the woods behind his house where he had seen rabbits many times. Within good view of the trap, he climbed a tree, made himself as comfortable as possible, and waited.

Two hours later a rabbit with a hop Johnny noticed was peculiar nosed by the trap. Soundlessly, Johnny waited. The rabbit entered the trap for the bait. The trap worked beautifully. Cheering, Johnny jumped from the tree and looked into the trap.

The rabbit was hunched over its front paws, twitching its nose. It did not appear frightened.

Johnny opened the trap and brought the rabbit to his lap. When he touched the rabbit's back right leg the rabbit twitched it away from him. With his fingers, Johnny could feel the leg was broken.

Johnny brought the rabbit back to the barn. He set and splinted the rabbit's leg. Then he built a commodious cage for it and put all sorts of good things in it: soft blankets, a dish of fresh water, lettuce and carrots from the garden. He would let the rabbit go when it was well.

That night at supper he told his mother he lost the sleeve of the sweater he was making, some dog ran away with it, and he was tired of knitting anyway.

Then he told her about trapping the rabbit and setting its broken leg.

"Maybe I'll be a doctor," he said.

By God, that tune has got my fingers tapping. *In the evening, in the evening, ump ump ump-a. . . .* If I'm so deaf, how come I remember tunes? I remember many of Amy's melodies. I seem to remember Bach was hard of hearing as he got along in years. I think he cheated, though. Used math. *Ump ump ump-a!* I wonder what happened to that straw hat of mine. That was a sweetie. It almost made up for those stiff collars that nearly choked me. How did we ever sing with those collars around our windpipes? Sing we did. Lustily. It would be growing dark. There would be the flies, of course. Around about eight or nine o'clock, just as it was getting really dark, the lamps would be lit in the house. Through the windows and the screen door yellow lamplight would pour out on us. *Shine on, shine on harvest moon. . . .*

Summer evenings Johnny in his straw hat would go to Elizabeth's house. Elizabeth lived on the main street just outside the center of town in the nicest house with the deepest front porch and the biggest lawn because her father ran the bank.

Elizabeth was the most beautiful girl in town and all the young people would go to her house on the especially wonderful evenings. Harry would bring his mandolin and Maud and Bobby would stop by during their walk and sit on the steps holding hands and Frances Mulvaney and Herbert Parker and Louise Swenson and the Pomeroys, brother and sister, would all come over and they would sit on the steps of Elizabeth's front porch and Harry would pluck the strings of his mandolin and they would sing all the old songs. There was a copper beech tree in Elizabeth's front yard and during these summer nights the breeze would go up through the thick, long leaves making a sound, and the youngsters without knowing it would take their pitch from the sound of the breeze in the tree and sing all the songs they could think of, trying some in harmony. All the houses around there had porches and the older people would sit on them in the twilight, in the swings and on the rockers, and they would listen to the youngsters singing. The cook at Elizabeth's house would be working the ice cream machine in the kitchen and she would be tapping her feet and humming some of those songs while she made the ice cream for the youngsters to have. Some of the young boys would be on the lawn trying their muscles out on each other, wrestling, or just making the dogs bark. Three-year-old George Brice, orphaned by a train wreck and then living with a young schoolteacher and his wife, also on the porch, used to sit on the sidewalk and imitate the singing in a high falsetto wail. Then the young ones would have to go home to bed and the evening would be full upon them all and the stars would be clear over the dark lawns and the trees and the roofs of the houses. The youngsters' singing would soften and the older folks on their porches would half smile, half cry at this crooning through the dark and the cook would slow the ice cream making down so the singing would not end too soon.

After a while the youngsters would have sung all the songs they could remember, and then some, and there would be quiet talking and the youngsters could hear the swings and rockers creaking from the other dark porches. Elizabeth and some of the girls would go in and help the cook dish out the soft ice cream and bring it out to the boys and the girls and the cook would stand in the doorway smiling down at the youthful silhouettes on the steps. The youngsters always thanked the cook for the wonderful ice cream and she would make some pleasantry, loving them, and then she would go up to her bed and read the latest thing from Street and Smith.

I wonder if I ever told Steve that I once heard the great John Philip Souza play. That was in Portland, the only place I went to medical conventions. I am very well traveled to medical conventions, in Portland, Maine. I skipped the lecture and went to the concert. That is my only musical distinction, other than having been the only person in the world outside her parents ever to hear Amy play. I should say they are two very considerable distinctions. Not everybody has the distinction of having been a lifetime audience of one. Add to that the distinction of having heard John Philip Souza and I'm not a bit sorry to have missed the rest of it. I never understood that much about music anyway. It's a fine way of communicating, though. Amy taught me that. I always suspected she must have known, or felt, someone was listening, that she was communicating with someone. She and John Philip Souza had much the same passion, the same excitement, the same urgency to make you feel something at the back of your neck.

Band music. Guess it's supposed to stir the blood, make people feel extra patriotic, make it easier for them to go off to war. That's what band music communicates, I guess: the excitement of war. I don't know if war is exciting, never been to one, but the music sure is exciting.

The postman came up the steps of the porch. He was sorting the mail in his hands.

"Were you in the war?" Doc John asked the postman.

"D Day."

"What?"

"The Normandy Invasion."

"Was it exciting?"

"Jesus."

"Like band music?"

"Not much, I don't."

"Mail?"

Doc John put his hand out for the mail but the postman pretended not to see him and put it in the box. Doc John put his hand back in his lap.

Miss Slade opened the door enough to take the mail out of the box. She looked at the letters.

"How's Miss Holly?" the postman asked her.

"I'm terribly afraid. I don't think she'll last the afternoon."

"We were just talking about the war," Doc John said.

"Anything I can do?" the postman asked.

"Nothing any of us can do."

"She's too young for it," the postman said.

"She's just fifty-seven." Miss Slade looked through the door at Doc. "He's eighty-seven."

The postman said, "Damned shame, if Miss Holly dies."

"And with a voice like hers," Miss Slade said. "She never missed a Sunday in her life. Gave inspiration to a lot of us."

"What would the old Doc do without her? He's pretty well gone, isn't he?"

"That's the irony of it. We've all been expecting him to die, every day."

"That's life," the postman said.

Miss Slade said, "That's life."

She went back into the house with the mail.

The postman said to Doc, "Read any good books lately?"

He had noticed it was always the same edition of *The Reader's Digest* on the Doc's lap, and usually the same edition of the newspaper.

"Say," Doc said. "Did you ever hear the Rebel song, *The boys in gray are marching, See the blue boys run!*"

The postman said, "You can't sing as well as Miss Holly, either."

"*The boys in gray are firing, See the blue boys run! Oh, how the blue boys run! The blue boys, the blue boys run!*"

"You should have seen the boys on Omaha Beach run, old man."

"I learned that ditty years and years ago, when I was a child. I still remember it."

"Yeah, well, don't forget that one. That's a good one."

"Was there any mail for me?"

The postman shook his head. "No," he said. "There's never any mail for you. It's all for Miss Holly."

"Oh. What time is it now?"

"Eleven."

"What? Oh, I heard you. Yes, sir. Lovely morning."

"Fine morning. Miss Holly would be singing when she came to the door a morning like this."

"Eh, eh," Doc chuckled. "That's right."

" 'That's right.' Doubt you were ever aware she sang. No one ever saw you in church. The good Lord's waitin' on you, old man."

The postman went down the steps.

"Don't forget to close the gate," the old man said. "See you tomorrow."

The postman closed the gate and went on to the next house.

Hello, there, little feller. You like the way you're perched on the porch rail? Of course you do. Hello. Would you like some bread? Some bread crumbs? I haven't got any bread crumbs. No, I'm sorry. I haven't. No bread crumbs at all for such a nice little bird. You're a sparrow, aren't you? A nice little sparrow. Steve probably wouldn't know if you were a sparrow or a pigeon. If he goes to the city he'll see lots of dirty old pigeons and no nice little sparrows like you. I'll ask Holly for some bread. "Holly? Holly?" Just you wait a minute. Holly will bring you some nice little bread crumbs for me. Such a nice little bird. You would come right over and eat out of an old man's hand, wouldn't you? Why not? I've never hurt a nice little bird like you. Why would I? "Holly? Holly?" All right, fly off. Good bye, little bird.

Doc John had had to go out on a call during the night and when he got back he remembered ruefully he had promised to go duck hunting with the Judge. He had been postponing going hunting with the Judge for years. There was no time to go back to bed.

In the cold darkness of the early morning he got dressed in his heaviest work clothes and waited out front for the Judge to pick him up. The headlights of the Judge's Pierce Arrow came around the corner of the quiet street. The car made a lot of noise in the early morning silence. The two men drove out to the ponds. They talked and the dog moved around in the back seat.

They sat in the blind two hours, watching the day become a lighter gray. It did not become any warmer sitting there next to the pond. The Judge had brought a shotgun for Doc and Doc sat with it over his knees, his hands folded over the black metal of the gun barrels. Mostly, he watched the dog. The Judge had set out the decoys and sat there, smoking. He would not talk, except in whispers. The Doc wanted to holler after two hours of this silent cold waiting.

Finally, the birds came down, quacking and flapping their wings on the water's quiet surface. The Judge became excited. He moved around in the little space trying not to step on John.

"Here, now, John," the Judge said in a loud whisper. "Shoot!"

"Me? No, you shoot. I'll watch how you do it."

"Pin one in the water and then take one in the air. Hurry up!"

To John the flapping and babble on the pond's surface indicated a society too lively to but admire. He raised the shotgun. The gray pond was spotted with the dark figures of the sitting ducks. It was hard for John to shoot between them.

"Missed," said the Judge. The sound of the shot sent the birds flapping up into the air. "Quick! Get one in the air before they all get away!"

"Oh. Yeah."

John raised the shotgun again and aimed at a clear space in the sky and squeezed the left trigger quickly before anything had a chance to fly into that clear space.

"Damn, you missed," said the Judge.

Doc John looked at the shotgun. "Glad my life doesn't depend on it."

In the Pierce Arrow on the way back to town the Judge told Doc John he had done fine, first time. He had gotten off a couple of pretty good shots. It was the light that was bad. Also, the birds were getting smarter every year. The Judge knew that for a fact. Clearly, Doc John had the instincts of a fine duck hunter. Now that he had discovered how enjoyable duck hunting was the Judge would look forward to going out with him again the next year. Maybe John would even think of investing in his own shotgun.

Doc John said, "Yeah," and stroked the head of the dog on the car seat beside him.

I've always wanted to see an ostrich walk. You'd think I would have seen an ostrich in a zoo or something. I would not care too much about seeing an ostrich walk in a zoo. I would like to see an ostrich walk on those long legs across a field. I've seen sandpipers walk. There are plenty of those right here in Columbia Falls. They're good to see walk, their little legs flickering over the sand. They're probably just as good to see walk as an ostrich. I would still like to see an ostrich walk, though. It would be like seeing two great, tall pine trees walking. I would like to see those two big pine trees up on Tatie Hill walk.

Those are two fine trees. I often wondered if those trees, standing there in their immutable silence and dignity, ever found a way of making love to each other. I've always wondered if they reached out their limbs to each other, embraced, and entwined their trunks around each other, in the dark, when no one was looking.

The trunks of the two trees ran up clear against the sky, taller than any trees around. The only branches and pines were at the very top; they looked like wide-brimmed hats on the long, gracefully curving trunks. Some big birds had their nests in the tops of those trees and their dark figures would sail in and out, climbing up the sky to their nests and then soaring down from them.

Anna attended school with the rest of the youngsters but none could be friendly with her. Her father was unknown; her mother spoke French Canadian, a little broken English; they lived in a small, unpainted house in the back of town. Her mother did much of the town's washing in a metal tub, outdoors on nice days. The house always was surrounded by clotheslines drooping with the town's drawers, petticoats, sheets and shirts.

At school, Anna wore whatever clothes were available to her that morning. The other youngsters recognized Anna's clothes as their own cast-off laundry. For some reason, it made them feel sick. They wondered whose former underwear she was wearing on any given day.

Elizabeth and her schoolmates could not bring themselves to speak to Anna when they were young and later they found they did not know her to speak to.

During the days when John's southern accent made the other youngsters consider him a roadshow he noticed Anna and his Adam's apple at the same moment. She was further developed than other girls her age. Her skin gleamed as if oil had been rubbed in it. John could see her clothes slipping off her skin, suddenly, because of its smoothness, leaving her nude before him.

John touched Anna in the school corridor, almost without knowing he was doing so. Anna gave him a long look. They went to the pharmacy for an ice cream sundae. Once in a while when he was out wandering over the hills of Columbia Falls she would appear from nowhere, just come up behind him, and they would walk along together. They seldom said anything. For a long time, it seemed, they looked at each other closely through each other's clothes, watched how each other moved in clothes, stretched them, filled them, were slim and muscular in them.

A summer night when they were very young they met somehow in the road as if they were magnetized to each other and wordlessly walked out of town to the base of Tatie Hill. There was a great full moon and it hung between two tall trees as if strung from them.

They stopped.

John began to stab the toe of his boot into the dirt of the road. He looked up Anna's body, her skirt and sweater, and then up Tatie Hill, up the two trees to the sky. He felt her hand against his trousers.

He took her hand and led her up Tatie Hill. Between the two trees, beneath the moon, he yanked off his shirt and faced her. She knelt and began to unlace his boots. As she did so, he leaned over and pulled off her sweater. He put the palms of his hands on her shoulders, on that skin gleaming in the moonlight, let them slip off her shoulders to her arms, and lifted her up, bringing her face to his, his mouth to hers. Then the skin of her breasts was against the skin of his chest and shortly the bones of their hips were against each other, and moving.

Good thing Anna's mother taught her how not to get pregnant. She didn't speak English too well but she communicated what she knew to Anna. The woman had made a natural mistake. I guess, in having Anna, and she made sure Anna would not make the same mistake. All those years Anna and I made love, all over town, on Tatie Hill, in the big closet of the Grange Hall, even in the churchyard, it almost seems in any dark spot that wasn't wet, we never did become the town scandal. Of course the Olson girl and her boy were not a scandal either, years later. Maybe I loved them so, had such joy in their happiness, because I'd had so much joy in Anna and myself at that age. We're all just birds in the trees, you know, doin' what's natural. Never could see the point of puttin' people in clothes or birds in zoos. We were so very young. Sure, people noticed the marks of passion on our faces and necks and sometimes commented on my skin condition, asking what it was, wondering if it was some strange form of acne. I was the only boy in town who never had acne. And I didn't play sports, either. No need to play sports when you're getting that much exercise. Oh, yes, Anna and I kept each other in beautiful physical condition. We had real enthusiasm for it. Folks in Columbia Falls couldn't have been too passionate, come to think of it, not to notice signs of hot passion among two of its town young. People hardly were aware Anna and I knew each other, spent time together. Our love-making we did out of public view, of course. Truth is, when we met in front of other people we had nothing to say to each other. We never had anything to say to each other anyway. Our bodies did all our talking for us. And I'd like to say that was plenty enough, but as things worked out, I guess it wasn't. In a way we truly didn't know each other at all.

When I came back from the teaching hospital, medical college, Anna had upped and married that bastard, Jackson. She never did say why. I never asked her. Just the way things were. We had never talked about marriage. We had never talked about anything.

I met her outside the hardware store.

Anna said, "You're a doctor now, John."

"In some ways, I am. Only in some ways."

"That's good. It's wonderful you're a doctor."

"You married Jackson?"

"Yes, John. I married Jackson."

Flushing, I asked. "How's that?" I only knew Jackson as a foul-mouthed roadhouse fistfighter from out back of the beyond. He never did much to earn money. How he kept himself so physically dirty without ever working was a town puzzle.

Anna lowered her eyes. "It's terrible, John. Just terrible."

I didn't have another conversation with Anna for about seven years.

How do things happen in life? Elizabeth was the most beautiful and popular young woman in town. I truly loved her, always. And she loved me, in her way, always. I was the young doctor in town. What happened is that the town virtually elected us to marry each other. That's how things happen.

I married Elizabeth.

And that was after her daddy's bank had collapsed and the family had lost everything, even that big white house with the copper beech and the lawn and that wonderful deep porch down the street.

I regret never having seen an ostrich walk. Maybe Steve will get to see an ostrich walk, someday, someplace, in its natural habitat. That would be wonderful for him. The things I have seen and the things I have not seen. I have not seen the ostrich but I have seen the sparrow and the sandpiper and the seagull and the dirty gray pigeons when I was in the city at medical college. It is great fun seeing a sandpiper walk. I would rather have lived life without seeing the pigeon, though. The pigeon is an animal demeaned.

I spent so much time watching the pigeons when I was in medical college I demeaned myself.

"Do you have any idea what we're talking about?" Frank Pomeroy asked.

"No. I don't."

Albert said, "You don't really belong here, Jack. In medical school."

Frank Pomeroy was also from Columbia Falls, Maine. He had big plans for himself, to practice medicine in Boston, Massachusetts, which plans he fulfilled, dying rich at forty-nine.

John Lambert and Frank Pomeroy had agreed to share rooms while at the teaching hospital in Boston. After a while a third man lived with them, Albert Duchamp. Pomeroy pointed out that having Duchamp live with them would lower their expenses. John Lambert suspected Frank Pomeroy wanted Albert Duchamp to live with them so Frank Pomeroy could have someone to talk with who would understand what he was saying.

John Lambert understood little of what either of them said.

He had not done well at Latin in school and had had no German, which was important in the studying of any science in those days. John simply could not master the medical vocabulary. He had had as much mathematics and chemistry and biology as anybody and he understood the drawings and the diagrams in the books and the demonstrations of the professors, especially in anatomy, but the lectures meant little to him. His notebooks were full of doodles. A professor would make some joke in Latin and the rest of the class would laugh and John would feel a wave of sleepiness come over him. He would walk out to the park and sit on a bench and watch the pigeons picking around the gray sidewalk scrounging for food. He hated them. He wanted to go home and hide in the hollow and listen to Amy play her wonderful stories on the piano. He wanted to take Anna to Tatie Hill or even to the big broom closet of the Grange Hall, work his mouth over every inch of gleaming skin on her body and tighten his every muscle against her every tightened muscle and come together as he believed only they could. He wanted to visit Elizabeth in her house and have hot chocolate and cookies with her by the fire. He missed Columbia Falls. He missed himself, the self he knew. He was pretty sure he could understand medicine but he was also pretty sure he would never understand medical language.

The first day came for them to be taught by the head of the teaching hospital, Doctor Brougham. They were to watch him cut up a human cadaver. Green, Pomeroy left the operating theater for some air. Duchamp threw up on the floor, as did some of the others. Unperturbed, Doctor Brougham continued. He pretended not to notice. He also pretended not to notice the steady interest and enthusiasm of John Lambert. By the end of that first session, John was assisting the doctor.

As time went on, the others shirked their emergency room duties. John worked double and sometimes triple shifts. He was in his element. There was the woman who had stabbed herself in her belly with a hat pin rather than have another baby. The old alcoholic who would come in nearly every night to tell John conflicting tales about his boyhood in the Wild West. The shame-faced father who had been shot in anger by his eight-year-old son. The ten-year-old boy dying of dehydration in a teeming city not lacking water. The baby girl with rectal bleeding no one could stop, even for minutes after her death. The young immigrant male in tight clothes who came in badly beaten and jumped to his death from a hospital window during the night. The boxer who had had both his eyes gouged out during an illegal fight, and said he held no grudge. The starving, homeless children from the street who came in because they were sick with an accumulation of everything, had had it with life at their early ages. The old man who brought his old wife he knew was dying to the hospital and went away, leaving her there, as if bringing her back from whence she came, returning her, unable to afford either her medical or funeral expenses. John accomplished marvels under the sometimes watchful eye of Doctor Brougham, wandering around fixing the bruises, breaks, lacerations. Whereas Pomeroy and Duchamp and the others would insist on taking detailed medical histories even sometimes when the emergency did not permit the time, John would look and touch and listen and sometimes decide, act with life-saving swiftness.

"Medicine isn't just guess work," Albert would say to John.

"You have to know what you're doing," Frank would add.

"I know what I'm doing," John would say.

"It's better to know why the patient died," Frank Pomeroy would say slowly and seriously, "than to take a chance at making a mistake."

After the most important written examination John scurried to the park and dropped onto the bench, his bench, the bench he hated most. The pigeons, the birds he hated most, came to coo around his feet. John Lambert felt as if he had just seen the worst accident conceivable, far worse than anything he actually ever had seen at the hospital, the worst mess of human blood and bones there could ever be. He felt shocked and sick. Images of Columbia Falls had been fading from his memory, the melodies Amy played, the passions of Anna, the comforts of Elizabeth. Now he would have to return to Columbia Falls, all this time wasted, not having accomplished what he had set out to do. Frank Pomeroy ultimately would return to his family, the town, a graduated, licensed doctor. Perhaps Mister Twombley would let John clerk in his hardware store. John remained on his bench until it was dark and cold.

"Doctor Brougham wants to see you," Albert said.

Frank watched John from across the room.

"I'll go right away," John said. He had planned to pack.

He went out again.

Doctor Brougham never sat down. He paraded his office, looking at John and away from him, making John feel his presence and his rejection. He made John sit down.

"John Lambert, you're a cheater."

"Yes, sir."

"What? Speak up."

"Yes, sir. I cheated. You are right, sir. Doctor. I cheated on the written examination."

"You didn't even cheat well," Doctor Brougham said, as if offended.

"No, sir. I knew I would get caught."

"Were you thus expressing contempt for your examiners? For the science of medicine? Or for yourself?"

"I, uh, I was just packing to go home, sir."

"Where is that? Where's home?"

"Columbia Falls, Maine, sir."

"Where on God's green earth is that? No, don't tell me. Don't tell me because I never want to hear of it again."

"No, sir."

Doctor Brougham flipped a paper on his desk with his fingernail. "Your marks have been dismal throughout."

"Yes, sir."

"Have you been cheating all along?"

"Sometimes."

"What? Speak up!"

"Sometimes, sir. When I had to."

"When you 'had to.' You cheated not to be outstanding, but just enough to scrape by, eh?"

"Yes, sir, I guess that's what I did. I understand well enough, sir. I've just never been able to master the medical vocabulary, the language. I mean, I can deal with things, diagnose, fix things without knowing their names. I find I can do that."

"Oh, shut up."

"Yes, sir."

"I've watched you work, Lambert, in the hospital, particularly the emergency room. You're a fine cheater."

"Sir?"

"Your methods are sometimes crude and appear thoughtless, in fact, I might even say frightening, but your results frequently are superb. I've seen you cheat pain and permanent grief and death scores of times. Many times I have been tempted to ask you if you have known what you are doing, but I have restrained myself because I knew you would not be able to tell me. I have just watched you go ahead and cheat like hell. Usually, your cheating has worked out."

"Sir?"

"You are going home, young Lambert, to wherever on God's green earth that is—"

"Columbia Falls, Maine, sir."

Brougham raised his hand. "I said I never want to hear those words again! Because I never want to hear of you again! Right now whether you get your medical degree and license for general practice depends solely upon me. And I am going to grant you that degree and that license. I am sending you home, young Lambert, to your small town in the Maine woods, to cheat. To cheat sickness, misery, maiming, pain, grief, and, when you can, death. The bog from which you come doubtlessly needs a cheater. It will get none better. That fop-in-jay, Pomeroy, with whom I believe you domicile, is also from your hometown, but he will never go back there, except to strut. I'm sending you back there, to cheat. Do you understand me? And if I ever hear of you being anywhere else, working near a city where real doctors practice, or anywhere near a qualified hospital, I shall swoop down upon you like an avenging angel, pluck you up by my talons, and drop you in a pot of boiling oil. I shall ruin you! Do I make myself clear?"

"Yes, sir. Doctor."

"Get out of my sight. Go and cheat death, as you can."

"Yes, sir."

Quivering, John got up and rattled toward the door.

"Lambert?"

"Yes, sir?"

"Do you believe in God?"

"No, sir."

"Why not?"

"I've seen the babies die."

"I see. Then I suppose it's perfectly all right for you to cheat. Just cheat better than you did today."

I've been a pretty good cheater, too. Cheated death lots of times. Some would say I'm still cheatin' death, I suppose.

I've been a silent doctor, though, some might even say taciturn. Elizabeth never could understand why I never did talk much about my work. I've offered very few explanations, during my career. People would ask me this and that and I'd put that expression on my face to indicate it was all too complicated for a lay person to understand. I got pretty good at making that face. I never had the language to tell them. As coroner, having to get up and testify in court nearly killed me. Sometimes I'd make up words that sounded Latin to satisfy Judge and jury that I knew what I was talking about. Having been cheated out of a medical degree, the kind that could stand Doctor Brougham's sworn testimony, by a lack of academic ability, I have done a lot of cheating to compensate. Good thing there weren't state boards and committees to license one in those days. I never would have made it. Doctor Brougham must have had a little bit of the cheater in himself. I have never hesitated to cheat, to do what was simple, humane, what worked, what I thought was best for all, and the number of times the results were bad you could put in a piss jar.

Yes, sir, people who are cheated one way or another cheat others and sometimes themselves and sometimes it's a good thing, some-times not.

In the case of me and Columbia Falls, Maine, I expect it was a good thing. Thanks to Doctor Brougham. Never saw him again, of course. Never saw Albert Duchamp. Never dared go back to class reunions. Only saw Frank Pomeroy a few times, when he came home to strut, until his parents died. I've hardly ever dared leave Columbia Falls, Maine.

Yes, sir, I am well traveled.

I am well traveled to medical conventions—in Portland, Maine.

Is that Steve? I can't be sure, right away. Goddamn, I'm going to keep cheating on this particular medical history, my own, as long as I can.

Steve came up the steps.

"Is it lunch time already?" the old man asked. "Time goes so fast. I've just been sitting here all morning reading and thinking. Time does go fast."

"What did you read, old fart? The history of a perfectly wasted life in the sticks?"

"Steve, do you know which is the sparrow?"

"The sparrow is the one that flies."

"You ought to know your birds, Steve. Everyone should know his birds."

"You should know some of the birds I've known, old fart."

"Do you like to watch the sandpiper skip along the beach? Eh?"

"You're pretty birdy yourself. Coo-coo."

"What?"

"I said, screw the birds!"

Smiling, Steve shook his head, *No*. He wore the expression of one who thought the topic was beneath his attention.

"Oh, I was just wondering. I've always wanted to see an ostrich walk."

"He's always wanted to see an ostrich walk. God! Why don't they take old people out and shoot them?"

"It would be something. Pigeons are not very nice to see. You wouldn't like the pigeons you see in the city. So dependent. They're beggars. But to see the way a sandpiper flits along the sand is something to see. To see the way an ostrich walks must really be something."

Shaking his head, Steve reached for the screen door handle. "Ostriches. He wants to see an ostrich walk. Crazy old fart!"

"Don't go in yet, son. Wait until you're called. Lunch isn't ready yet. Did you ever hear that rebel song, Steve, the one that goes, *The boys in gray . . . The boys in gray . . .* I could remember it this morning. How does it go now?"

"The boys in gray are screwing in the hay, tra la."

"*The boys in gray . . .* I could remember it this morning. I sang it all through for the postman."

"I'll bet he was thrilled."

"Well, it's slipped my mind now. I'll sing it to you when I think of it. I sang it all through for the postman. You know I delivered him? Isn't that funny? Being so old a doctor I can say I delivered the postman! He certainly has grown into a sizable parcel!"

"Lunch," Steve said. "LUNCH!"

No one had called him to lunch. He went into the house.

"I'll write it down next time it comes to mind and then I'll sing it to you. He's gone in. Must be lunchtime. Let me see. *The boys in gray, de dum de da de dum . . .*"

4

Miss Slade came out onto the porch with a tray. "Here's some lunch for you, Doc."

"Thank you very kindly."

"Some light soup and bread. Just what an old man like you needs. Keeps up your strength."

"That's good, that's good."

"You just holler when you're through and I'll bring your tray back into the kitchen."

"That so?"

"The old fool can't hear a word I say. I SAY I'LL COME GET YOUR TRAY. JUST HOLLER WHEN YOU'RE THROUGH."

"When?"

"WHEN YOU'RE THROUGH."

"Today? Is that so."

"Merciful heavens, he can't hear a word I say. I'll just have to remember to come get the tray."

"Can I have a cigarette?" the old man asked.

"No. They're bad for you."

"After I eat my lunch?"

"No. NO. THEY'RE BAD FOR YOU."

Miss Slade went back into the house, pulling the screen door tight so the flies wouldn't get in.

Quite a set of tits on that old woman. When I was a medical student we used to know what to do with nurses with tits like that. Seldom if ever did it, though.

No taste to this soup from a can. No taste to anything anymore. Everything comes from cans and packages. One day they'll put tits in packages too, sell them down at the supermarket. Hardly worth having a mouth, these days.

Maybe Janey Slade will give me a cigarette later. She certainly ought to. Came to my office when she was in high school. Asked me how she could go about becoming a nurse. Her folks had no money. I helped her apply. Recommended her. Paid her tuition. After she did a stint at City Hospital she wanted to come home. I created the job of town nurse for her. All that ought to be worth a cigarette.

She got to meet Doctor Brougham, too, at City Hospital. He would have been pretty old, by then. So he did get to hear the words *Columbia Falls, Maine,* at least once more in his life. I doubt he remembered his aversion to those words.

I doubt he remembered me.

I wonder what Miss Slade would say if I told her I'm not really a doctor; I never passed my exams honestly. I've been cheatin' all my life. She might agree I've done a good job, cheatin'. She should know.

I wonder what she's doing here all day and all night. At first I thought it was me they were watching. I guess I'm old enough to be worthy of such attention. It would be just like her to move in because she thought I was sick. Sweet kid. But I guess it's Holly. She must be pretty sick. Of course you can be pretty sick when you're young and come through it all right. She'll be all right. Probably has a touch of the flu or something, only nowadays they call it the virus. Sounds more Latin for them. Virus is the new package they put that particular bug in. All she probably needs is a good dose of salts, a good cleanout. They ought to ask my advice. But they don't think of me. I'm too old to be thought of, as a regular thing. I used to take some long cold rides to their houses in the middle of the night. They thought of me then. Hell, I brought nearly everybody within shoutin' distance into this world, whether they like it or not. Kept them here, too, sometimes against their wills.

If Elizabeth were here, we wouldn't need Miss Janey Slade. Elizabeth would know what to do. There would be no need for public nurses with Elizabeth and me around. She would put taste into this soup, for one thing, and the mere fact of taste would make us all perk up mighty fast.

I'm dropping half this soup into my pants. Cheatin' soup: it's taking a short cut. So what. Hope Steve doesn't see my pants are wet. He'll think I've lost control of more than my hands.

Elizabeth was an all right cook. None of this packaged stuff. She made some fine things: cakes, pies, all sorts of baked goods. There was always a piece of cake or pie for me whenever I came in late, wherever I had been. She always had a chicken for Sunday dinner. Every Sunday of our married life, she had a roast chicken for dinner. You could count on it. She used to laugh, when people were present, the way 'Doc' used to cut the chicken. I was never very good at it. Not natural, to cut into a beast that way with a carving knife, slice off strips of it. She always thought my discomfort at cuttin' a chicken funny.

I wonder if Elizabeth would use packaged foods if she were alive today. Probably. Female nature degenerated the minute someone invented packaged food. Working hard over food takes love. Gardening, shopping, bringing raw food up into something pretty and tasty makes a woman aware of her love for the people she feeds. And them for her. Packages make people aware of nothing but the clock. The new method of preparing food abbreviates women's work. It abbreviates a woman's love.

Of course, Elizabeth wouldn't package her tits, either. They weren't on the market at all. I always knew she loved me, though, despite that, from the way she cooked and kept house for me. She cooked well, and there was much love in the things she turned out.

In the bedroom of his own house, John waited for his wife. Elizabeth was downstairs feeding Holly her formula. John kept giving himself things to do in the bedroom, straightening his shirt drawer, then his sock drawer so he would appear busy, at least not be in bed, when she came in. She had been saying it was too soon after Holly's birth. He was a doctor, and he knew. She kept saying she did not feel like it just yet. He rearranged his neckties on the closet rack. He listened to her climb the stairs and put Holly in the crib in the little bedroom next to theirs.

That night he hoped to be romantic.

When Elizabeth came into the bedroom she looked at him as she walked past him and got into her side of the bed. He knelt on the bed and studied her face. That look had meant everything to him.

"Are you angry?" he asked.

"No."

He lay on his side, putting his chin near her shoulder and his knees against her hip. She moved her hips an inch away. He put his hand gently on her breast.

Looking to the ceiling, she sighed.

"What's the matter, Elizabeth?"

"I've just had a baby," she said.

"So. Ten weeks ago."

There was a teardrop in her eye near her nose. She worried her lower lip with her teeth.

"You did not have a hard time having the baby, Elizabeth, but I know you did not enjoy it."

She said, "John, I do not want to make love again. Ever. In any way. I do not enjoy it."

"Elizabeth . . . " John sat up on the bed. "Elizabeth?"

"I've given you a child, John."

Through the bedroom door he could see the long, dark corridor leading to the stairs down to the front door. "You can't be serious."

She took a handkerchief from a table her side of the bed and dried her eyes. "I don't like sex. I don't enjoy the activity."

He pulled in breath and nearly choked on it. "That's all? That's it?"

"Yes, John. Please turn out the light."

John was thirty years old.

He never had carnal knowledge of his wife again.

I often thought of Elizabeth as being like the boy who is seven feet tall and insists he doesn't *like* basketball. One is sure he would be wonderful at it, even enjoy it, if only he'd try.

Elizabeth was disturbingly beautiful. She was the focus of any room or street she was in. All her life, boys and men would work their way across whatever room, whatever landscape to her. Once in front of her, their hands and feet, eyes and grins, would appear to triple in size. Maybe that was enough for her.

I know as a fact no one ever got anything more out of her.

Of course I was shocked, hurt, angry, mournful, all those words that mean nothing much when you're describing a healthy thirty-year-old male who has been refused sexually by his wife, especially when that healthy thirty-year-old male is a doctor in a small town who lives under a telescope peered into by the whole community, but I never meant to embarrass Elizabeth as I did.

Two or three months later, when I had to decide Elizabeth really was serious, that this was not a passing mood, I gave in to my anger or whatever. I had twin beds delivered to our house and set up in our bedroom. I sent our nearly new double bed to the Reverend and Mrs Harshburger, at the parsonage. I could not stand sleeping in the same bed with this beautiful woman I could not touch. It was difficult living in the same house with her. Of course, divorce was unthinkable at that time. Divorce would ruin a small town doctor. And there was no place else I could go, to practice. I did not realize the whole town would know I had sent our double bed to the parsonage a few months after our one and only child, Holly, was born, or that they would read correctly what that meant.

Elizabeth never said anything to me about my having given our bed away. Ever after, however, there was something chastized in her look.

Since then, a lot of kids have been born out of that bed. All the Harshburger kids, the Smoot kids. Who was the last kid born out of that bed I know of? Oh, yeah, little Danny Prescott. Nice boy. Steady eyes. No one will ever get away lying to him. Great coloring. Cute little body for a boy, instantly, insistently male. Lots of nice kids born out of that bed over the years. None of them mine.

Celibacy might have made a better doctor out of me. At least, it turned me into a very hard-working, very efficient doctor. I never minded getting called out at night. Somehow single beds are easier to leave. In fact it gave me trivial satisfaction that Elizabeth would get awakened frequently by something having to do with me. Either I thought about my work, hard, all the time, even read the medical journals, or, I was convinced, I would go crazy. Maybe I wasn't a better doctor. I lost some of my empathy, became a much harder man. The human became much more clinical to me, a mass of struts and pipes, and I became more of a carpenter and plumber. I began to act and think completely in accordance with gray community standards, never expecting a heavy burst of rain or unadulterated sunshine. I turned cynical, jaded. Not a better doctor, no, a worse doctor, but a doctor who knew more and thought more academically.

One relates to a small community. It has its ways of teaching you things, of always bringing you around to yourself. I say a *small community:* maybe I mean the world.

By Gar. The Olson family. The ever-enlarging Olson family.

A burst of unadulterated sunshine.

Olson was sitting on the edge of a chair in the waiting room, with his cap in his hands, picking at it, when Doc John returned from a call. Olson's big, blond face was concentrating on a frown.

Doc John seldom had seen Olson in town.

"Doctor," Olson said, jumping up, "my wife, I'm afraid for our baby. Something is wrong with her. Her stomach." Olson's big hand described a distended stomach. "Always good food at my house. Can you come please look at her?"

"It's a long way out to your farm. Why didn't you bring the baby in?"

Olson shook and scratched his head at the same time. "Too far, Doctor, in the wagon. She's really sick, the baby."

The Olsons lived in a community of Swedish farmers so far out of town eventually they would declare themselves a separate town.

"Okay."

Olson drove out with Doc John in the Winslow.

"Near death, Doctor. Sonja's never been sick, not one day. Always good food at my house. Plenty of it. Now my baby is very sick. Won't eat."

Again Olson's hand described a swollen stomach.

Doc John drove a long way, over increasingly narrower and bumpier dirt roads. He never would have found the neat farm in the hills if Olson hadn't shown him the way.

Olson's wife waited at the front door. A fat woman, she was wringing her hands in her apron. "Sonja, Doctor. Our Sonja!"

"Where is she?"

The obese Mrs Olson showed Doc John into the parlor.

The most beautiful young girl John had ever seen came into the sunlit parlor, lighting it up even more. Fully developed, strongly built, with long, curly blond hair, she had the most enormous blue eyes. Her face was tanned and the skin of her nose was peeling a little from the sun.

She was smiling shyly at the doctor.

"Where's the baby?" John asked.

"Sonja." Olson looked fondly at the girl. "The baby."

John had to try hard not to laugh. "Olson, you're right. Is there somewhere I may, uh, examine Sonja?"

Olson's wife showed them to a bedroom on the first floor.

Sonja sat on the bed. She began to remove her shirt.

"Stop that," John said, standing over her. "Stop it." The girl's huge eyes bulged at him. "How old are you?"

"Fourteen, Doctor."

"Who do you think you're kidding?"

"I kid no one."

"Who is he? Your father?"

The girl looked toward the closed bedroom door. "Who's who?"

"The man who did this to you?"

"Did what?"

"You've been with a man," Doc John said.

Sonja appeared to be trying to remember. Slowly, she said, "No. I don't think so. Yes, I work with my father, in the barns, the fields. The chickens—"

"Sonja, we're not talking about chickens."

She turned her gorgeous face up to him. "What are we talking about, Doctor?"

"You're pretty isolated out here."

"What does 'isolated' mean?"

John was distracted by something that flashed in the window.

"Sonja, believe me, I understand. But I need to know. Has your father ever touched you?"

"Of course! Of course he touches me. All the time he touches me."

"I mean, kissed you, hugged you?"

"Of course, Doctor. Why not?"

"You're about to find out why not." Again, John got the impression of something flashing in the window, just for a second, not by the window, but up and down in it. "What's that?"

Sonja looked at the empty window. "What's what?"

"I thought I saw something."

Head down, Sonja said, "My mother loves me, too."

That time, John definitely saw something in the window, yellow hair, tanned skin, and big blue eyes.

He opened the window more, leaned out and looked down. A boy was crouched in the flower bed.

John reached down and grabbed him by his hair. Then he got ahold of him under his armpits. John lifted the boy up and through the window into the room.

"Oh," Sonja said. "That's Lars."

Instantly, Lars sat on the bed next to Sonja. He took her hand.

"Sonja, what is the doctor saying? What is he saying is wrong?"

"Is Lars your brother?" John asked.

Except for their ages the two children could have been a twin. Even the sunburns on their noses matched.

Lars was not much more than half Sonja's size. Shoulder muscles were just beginning to appear beneath his shirt.

"No. He lives on the farm next." She waved her arm over the back hill.

"Sonja, what's wrong?" Lars asked.

"You know I'm sick in the mornings. Father does not like my not eating breakfast now. He says starvation has made my stomach swell. So he has gotten the doctor."

John said, "Starvation . . ."

"Oh," said Lars. "It's too bad that you are starving."

"Sonja," Doc John said. "You're not starving. You're pregnant!"

"Pregnant?" Sonja's eyes were each as big as the world. "Like the cow?"

"Cow," John said. "Chickens."

Lars' hand shot into the air. "We did it!" He jumped onto the bed and began jumping up and down on it. "Sonja! We did it!"

John said, "You?"

"We did it!" He fell to his knees, threw his arms around Sonja, and hugged her. Laughing, they fell over onto the bed.

John grabbed the laughing boy's arm and made him sit up. "How old are you?"

Giggling, the boy counted his fingers and added one. "Eleven, this year."

"Eleven!"

"We were very curious," Sonja said.

"We made a baby!" Lars ducked around Doc John and opened the bedroom door to the rest of the house. "We made a baby!" he yelled. "Sonja and I. We made a baby!"

Mrs Olson's girth filled the doorway. "Doctor, is this true?"

"If they say so."

Towering behind his wife, Olson asked, "She's not starving, Doc?"

"She's not starving."

"Will this be an okay baby, Doc? Will it be all right?"

John shrugged. "I don't see why not. They're not related. They're both healthy." He laughed. "They're both gorgeous!"

Sonja, still sitting on the bed, grabbed Lars' hand from the air, and held it. "It is lots of fun." She scanned her parents' and Doc's faces with her magnificent eyes. "I mean, what Lars and I do. With each other, I mean. When we get undressed, and hug each other."

John turned his back to the room for a moment. He blew his nose.

Olson said, "My baby made a baby!"

Arms outstretched, Mrs Olson flung herself at her daughter. "Sonja!" On the bed, mother and daughter rolled and hugged and laughed.

The boy, the eleven-year-old boy, laughing, fell safely on top of them. Arms around both women, he rolled and laughed with them.

"Gar!" Olsen stood over the bed putting his huge hands out to everyone, tickling his daughter, punching the boy, petting his wife. "My baby made a baby! With this young bull! This calf!"

His face buried in the women, his voice muffled, Lars said, "Bull!"

Doc John went back to the parlor to collect his black bag.

He heard a bell clanging loudly.

Looking through the parlor window to see who was ringing a bell, Doc John saw several towheaded children running toward the house. Olson stood on the back porch beating the bell even though everyone in sight was running already. One boy ran with a baby on his back. They ran from the vegetable garden and the barn and from around the corner of the milk shed. He counted them. Eight children, including the back-borne. There wasn't a slow or unsturdy one among them.

They burst into the house through several doors.

Instantly, the house was full of babble.

"Sonja? To have a baby?"

"Of her own?"

"Like the cow?"

"Lars had something to do with it."

"Lars! He's smaller than I am!"

In the parlor, Doc John found himself waist-high in blond, sunburned, farm-smelling, babbling children.

Olson, like a giant, stood among them, shaking his head. "Not starving, my Sonja! Pregnant!"

Sonja and Lars stood holding hands in the door. Lars' head was only as high as Sonja's shoulder.

Mrs Olson came through the parlor door with a pitcher and milk, a dozen glasses, and a plate of oversized cookies. Despite the big news, the children swarmed to her before she could set the tray on a table.

"Cookies, Doc?" Mrs Olson called.

"No. No, thanks."

Olson frowned. "Are you sick?"

"No, not sick. Please don't call another doctor!"

"Then eat something!"

John laughed. "Why the hell not?"

A child brought him a glass of milk and two cookies.

"By Gar." Again Olson shook and scratched his head simultaneously. "My baby has a baby."

"Sonja your oldest daughter?" Doc John asked.

"Yah!"

"You'd better buy more farms, Olson!"

"Yah!" Face filled with delight, Olson held his arms out wide. "More farm!"

Having left his horse and wagon in town, Olson had to drive back with the Doc. They had left Mrs Olson and her children and Lars dancing happily all over the house and front yard. All the way into town, Olson kept scratching and shaking his head, saying, "My baby has a baby. More farm!"

Life isn't like that. I know that well. Life does not burst with love and health and happiness. That is ideal, not real. But I saw the ideal, once. I did have that one moment with the Olson family. It was the ideal exception that proved the rule of reality to me.

I drove back to town happy and sad. That moment with the Olsons made a difference to me. I had driven out wondering what I was driving into, braced for another dying or dead baby. A messy farm. Bitter wife. There was nothing wrong at all, but I was quick to see wrong. A big husband, a fat wife, a beautiful, pregnant daughter. *Has your father ever touched you . . . I mean, kissed you, hugged you?* I almost traumatized the child. I had been reading too many medical journals, I guess. Children playing, curious about the animals, had got themselves pregnant. And they had enjoyed it. And in their little world out there, it was all right. *Yah! More farm!* It was a beautiful moment, for me, but it made the rest of time less beautiful.

It is better not to glimpse heaven, if one must return to earth.

Elizabeth kept a mighty fine house, too. She was house-proud. She had the lovely white window curtains just so and my pipes were always put away so that they were never where I left them. I never saw a speck of dust in my house in all my married years. She would make the beds almost before we were out of them.

Of course Holly took care of the house, and me, after Elizabeth died, just beautifully. It was just not the same. Things were never perfect again, the floors and furniture always looking just polished, the carpet fibers always standing up because a vacuum cleaner had just been run over them, the curtains just right in the windows, a piece of pie or cake always where you'd hope to find it. Holly insisted on keeping her job in the bank, and that was good for her, I suppose; it would not have been good for her to become full-time slave to an old man and a boy. We had Steve to raise. And Wednesday nights and Sunday mornings she'd disappear down to the church to hum with the rest of them. She did well but there was never the perfection, the devotion, the thoughtfulness in her cooking and housekeeping there was in Elizabeth's. How could there be.

There wasn't the guilt.

Miss Slade came out to take the tray away.

"May I have a cigarette?" the old man asked.

"Merciful heavens, how many times must I say no. No, no, NO, NO, N O."

"Later?"

"NO!"

"What harm would it do?"

She went back into the house, holding the screen door open with her posterior while she guided the tray sideways through the door. Inside, she put the tray on a table and pulled the screen door shut tight. Miss Slade was most particular about not letting flies into the house.

Where's Holly? Holly will let me have a cigarette. No reason why I should be bossed by a nurse. Never saw Doctor Brougham being bossed by a nurse. He'd stomp 'em. I never had the self-confidence, as a doctor, to stomp on a nurse.

"Holly? Holly?" She'll get me a cigarette.

It's always hard to know what to tell the young. My best story, about the Olsons, I'd never tell Steve. He might think that ideal life I saw out at their farm was natural, and that would just get him into trouble in the real world. I admit, remembering the Olsons once again has made me feel vaguely discontented. I tell myself it was an illusion. The Olsons just could not have been as I saw them, remembered them. The mind can play funny tricks on one, lie to oneself for a long time. As it did with me and Anna. I went out to the Olsons' farm expecting to see something and, at first, seeing it; but really needing to see something else, and, finally, seeing what I needed to see. Of course I'd never tell Steve about Anna, either: another illusion.

Old folks should keep their illusions to themselves.

Let the young create their own illusions.

"Holly?"

Steve came out, eating an apple.

"Hello, there, Steve," the old man said.

" 'Lo."

He sat down on the top step.

"Have a nice lunch?" the old man asked.

Steve stared into space as he munched his apple. He said, "Grand-dad, my mother is dying."

"Was it good?"

"Fine. Just lovely. The end of life is coming in on her in that little room in there and she is all alone, all alone in her head. Comatose. Goddamn it."

"Well, a growing boy like you ought to eat good food, lots of good food. You won't get fat. You'll burn it all off playing ball, you know. All you have to do at your age to stay strong is eat good food."

"She's a person. She must have been restless, too, gotten hot pants, seen things she didn't want to see, be things she didn't want to be. She must have wanted to be and do and have a lot of things she couldn't. Isn't that so?"

"Yes, yes."

"Talking to you is like talking to a head of lettuce." Steve hurled his apple core across the street, to the opposite curb. "I'll bet you want a cigarette, though."

"That's right, Steve."

Steve stood up and held his package of cigarettes out to the old man.

"Thank you very kindly, sir."

Steve lit both cigarettes.

"You know, Steve, I'm not really a doctor."

"Sure."

"One man had the right to give me my license to practice, or to withhold it, and he had every reason to withhold it."

"Right. You're not Doc Lambert now. You're Napoleon now, I suppose. And I'm George Washington."

"I've had to bluff my way through life. Cheatin', if you know what that word means. Cheatin' death."

"You sure have been cheatin' death."

"Steve," the old man said, "is your mother really sick?"

"Sick to death, as they say."

"What? I can't hear you, Steve."

Steve nodded his head, *Yes.*

The old man saw it.

"She'll be all right," Doc said.

"She'll be all right once she's dead. Jesus, the only way out of this town. Not for me. I'm going to live, before I die."

"She just probably needs a good cleaning-out."

"That's disgusting."

The old man saw the tears in Steve's eyes.

"You're a disgusting old man."

"You know, Steve, I can't hear everything you say."

"You're old. You've been old all my life. You've always been old!"

"That's right, Steve. That's right. The truth is, the world is a pretty good old place, once you get the hang of it. There are lots of good things in this life."

" 'Good things'! Jesus!" Steve flicked his cigarette stub into the bushes. "You old fart!"

He went down the steps and through the gate into the street.

"That's right, Steve. Just hang in there, however you can."

5

So Holly is really sick. I mustn't be sad, either. She'll be all right.

She's young and strong.

She can take it.

There are plenty of good things to think about. Who got married recently? Nobody I know. Ends that happy thought. Someone should get married. Maybe I'll marry that Miss Janey Slade. Not if she won't let me have cigarettes, I won't.

Once, when I was very young, in the south, I rolled down a long, steep, grassy slope, rolling around, around, around to the bottom. When I got up I felt dizzy and happy and had grass on my sweater. That's something to think about.

And music, of course, about which I know nothing. I've always liked it, though. Harry sure could play that mandolin. Never see mandolins around any more. Steve never wanted a mandolin. I don't remember twitching to the sound of a mandolin. I suppose we did.

Everything has its age, mandolins, knickers; you never see knickers around anymore, either. Everything has its age, mandolins, straw hats, knickers, and Doc John. Whatever happened to that Doc John? He was a nice enough fellow. Well, it's a long story. He got old. That's what happened to Doc John. He doesn't get around much anymore. That's what we used to say about old people. It was our courtesy. I suppose they still say it. Then they say, That's too bad. He was a nice enough fellow. They past-tense you before you are dead. They past-tense you right out of existence.

Whatever happened to that Anna Jackson? That's the question, isn't it.

I doubt she gets around much anymore, either.

Doc John's office was in a low, brick building next to the MacGregor Youth Center. There was a waiting room with wicker chairs and magazine tables. Inside there was an office with desk and chair; chairs facing the desk for visitors. Next to the inside office was a small examining room with a hat rack for patients to hang their clothes, an examining table, and the best lights Doc John was able to rig. In each room was a carpet he meant to be bright and cheery. Windows faced out onto the main street and Eliot's Grocery Store across the way.

At thirty-five, Doc John's life was relentlessly, purposefully busy. There was much need for him around Columbia Falls. From eight in the morning he would see patients in his office. After lunch with Elizabeth at home, he would spend his afternoons doing his rounds of the bedridden, making house calls, sometimes driving as much as fifty miles a day. When he returned to his office, usually in the early evening, he would try to take a few minutes for himself, straighten up his office, his records, sit at his desk and smoke his pipe. After a late dinner at home with Elizabeth, he would read his medical journals. Seldom was the night he did not get called out of bed to attend a stroke patient, a heart attack, a sudden, raging fever, a death, to deliver a baby.

At that time in his life, John did not want to see his bed with any better, more necessary idea in his head than to sleep.

One late afternoon, alone in his office, feet up on his desk, John was smoking his pipe. His mind reviewed his patients' conditions, his diagnoses, prognoses both public and private. During those days, Doc John had to remind himself almost daily that, to a patient, pregnancy, accident, illness, death were the major events of life. He saw so much of it he found it hard to share in his patients' perspectives. To him life seemed a running medical emergency. Sometimes he knew he saw the amputation of a farmer's mangled leg simply as something he did in an afternoon between delivering a baby and writing an old woman's death certificate.

When he heard someone in the waiting room he dropped his feet to the floor and banged the ashes out of his pipe. "Come in."

He was putting on his white jacket when he heard Anna's voice. "Hello, John."

She stood in the doorway of his office watching the way his body moved in his shirt.

She was dressed very badly, of course, like an old woman, in a dark, hanging long dress, sweater she could not button, a hat with a slightly torn brim, cracked black shoes. There seemed to be permanent blue marks on the left side of her face, on her cheekbone and forehead.

Otherwise, in the fading light from the window behind him, her skin gleamed as fresh as it always had.

He buttoned his jacket. "Well, hello. What's the matter with you today?"

"I've got some bruises," she said. "Will you look at them?"

"Where?"

"All over my body."

"Where did you get them?"

Her voice was low. "Jackson beats me. All the time."

He opened the door to his examining room, let her pass within, closed it. Then he closed the door to the waiting room.

When he entered the examining room she was not on the table or behind it. Naked, proud, her eyes steady in his, she was standing in about the only place in that small room her full body could be seen from the door.

"Anna." Her limbs were still slim, muscular, her breasts firm, her stomach flat, graced by a moderate Venus mound, her hips in wondrous proportion to her waist, her shoulders. And there was her wonderful skin, now blued here and there, on the front of one shoulder, over her left rib cage, her left forearm, her right hip, one thigh. "Get on the table please."

She moved like a cat onto the table.

John opened the window behind the closed drape.

Examining her, he said, "Why don't you leave him?"

"I haven't a nickel, John."

"I should think you'd know, or be able to guess, I have an extra few hundred dollars I could let you have."

"He'd find me. Sober, he's clever; drunk, he's violent. Sober, he'd find me. Drunk, he'd kill me. And the child."

"You have a child."

"A girl. Patty. A home birth, John."

"Why didn't you call me? It would have cost you nothing."

"Jackson had a woman in, from back country. He said childbearing is among women."

"You had some broken ribs."

"I know."

"They seem to have healed all right. And I suppose you know your right arm was broken."

"I bound it up with slats and clothesline. Jackson even beat me for that. For having a broken arm."

"Did he break it?"

"Of course."

"Anna, I don't see anything recent, anything that needs immediate attention." He kneaded her stomach. "Feel anything when I do this?"

"Of course, John. I feel your hands. Your wonderful hands. It's been a long time since I have felt your wonderful hands."

"I mean, does your stomach hurt in any way? Are you able to eat, digest without pain, function normally?"

"Yes."

John washed his hands at the little sink.

"Anna? Why did you come to see me? I mean, why did you come to see me now?"

She was sitting on the examining table, her legs over its edge.

"You had one child, John. Almost six years ago."

"Holly. Yes."

"Then you gave your double bed to the parsonage."

"I guess everyone in town knows that."

"Will you ever have more children, John?"

"I guess not."

"Why not, John? John, tell me the truth."

John wiped his forehead with the hand towel. "Elizabeth does not enjoy the activity."

"I've wondered."

"I shouldn't have said that."

"I see you in the street sometimes, walking with your little black bag, driving by. Your eyes don't look out any more. They look in. You do not smile."

"I've been pretty busy. Caring for a whole town—"

Anna's eyes were smiling. "Johnny ... your pants are bulging."

He did not need to look down. "Shut up."

He went into his office and filled his pipe. He was lighting it when Anna entered from the examining room. She was fully dressed in those terrible clothes.

John shook out his match. "You'd better not come here again, Anna."

"All right."

"Elizabeth loves me, in her way."

Anna smiled. "Jackson loves me. In his way."

"Of course, if you really need help, you or the child, I'm here."

Anna said, "All right, John."

I know why she came to my office that particular afternoon. She wanted sympathy and understanding, of course; I thought so then. I did not guess immediately at the rest of it.

She wanted to know if she could depend upon me. She either knew or had some idea of what was going to happen, what she was going to do. Maybe she knew perfectly well, or maybe she knew it was inevitable. She had her own future to provide for, and the child. She had to have someone. She came to me, as she should have. She asked me about my married life. I did not keep it from her that I was alone in many important ways. It would have done no good to lie to Anna. She knew me too well. She knew men too well. She had that very feminine instinct. Looking at a man, smelling him, she knew his needs. By the time she left my office, she knew exactly to what extent she could count on me.

That same night I had been in bed asleep for only about a half-hour when the telephone rang.

It was Anna. Her voice was shaking. At first she said Jackson had had an accident. She said she was calling from Teatle's Crossroads Store because Jackson had never put in a telephone. Of course he hadn't. Jackson hadn't put in plumbing. I tried to find out what had happened. Crying, Anna said the baby had been hurt. "Come quick," she said.

I dressed and drove out to Jackson's place. It was in a lane off the main road pretty far out of town, about a quarter-mile from Teatle's Crossroads Store. It was an unkempt frame house, surrounded by dark pine, and weeds. All sorts of junk, failed projects, were strewn all over the yard. Through the windows came the soft yellow light of kerosene lamps. More than one window was smashed.

Doc John did not wait for his knock to be answered.

Inside, Anna, looking like a startled animal, stood the other side of a wooden table. On the table was a kerosene hurricane lamp. In that light her eyes looked impossibly wide, dark, bright, frightened.

"Please, John."

Against the inside wall of the room a baby cried and waved her legs and left arm in a crib.

"Oh, please. John?"

Jackson lay on his back on the floor beside the table. The handle of a screwdriver was just above his left eye. The screwdriver had been driven into his head. Blood had fountained out of his eye for a goodly time before subsiding, stopping.

"John? Please."

There was an empty liquor bottle on the table, a spilled bottle on the floor, and a broken bottle in the crib.

"Her collarbone is broke."

"Patty. Oh, please, John."

"No lacerations to speak of. One minor cut, not bleeding. I don't know about internal injuries, of course. You all right?"

"John?"

"Here, sit down." He held a chair for her.

"I can't." Anna was holding onto her stomach.

"How hurt are you?"

"I'm not hurt. I'm sick. I was sick in the woods, going down to Teatle's."

"Anna, did he hit you in the stomach?"

"Of course. I'm not hurt."

"Do you taste blood?"

"He was hurting the baby, John."

"I understand." John dipped a coffee mug into a bucket of water near the back door and brought it to her. He shook pills out of a bottle from his black bag and handed her two. "Take these."

Anna tossed them into the back of her throat and gulped some water.

She began to cry hard. "John? John? The baby. Patty. Oh, please!"

"She'll be all right. It's over, Anna. Everything will be all right."

"What am I going to do? You know what happened, John."

"I expect I do."

"John? Oh, please, John."

"Anna? Look over at the baby."

"What?"

"Turn around. Look at the baby."

Crouching, John bent Jackson's right elbow. He squeezed Jackson's right fist around the handle of the screwdriver a moment. The blood helped it stick.

The rest John did with his foot. He flipped Jackson's body onto its stomach. He straightened the head, turning the face more toward the floor.

He pressed his shoe hard against the back of Jackson's head, driving the screw driver further into his brain.

"Okay. Anna, you and the baby have to come with me into town."

Anna studied Jackson's body. "What did you do?"

"Drunk, Jackson fell on his screwdriver. What was he doing, making a toy for the baby?"

With Anna and the baby in the car, I woke up the Teatles again and called the Chief of Police. Drunk, I said, Jackson had fallen and stuck his screwdriver through his eye. He was dead. I was taking Anna and the baby with me to my office and would bring them back to their house shortly after dawn. Patty did have a broken collarbone, which I straightened out in the good light of my office. There was nothing more wrong with Anna than there had been that afternoon. Once in the car, she calmed down considerably. I brought them both back to their house after seeing Anna and the baby had a good breakfast at Mrs Selfridge's coffee shop. The police and undertaker had been there and taken Jackson's corpse away and cleaned up all the evidence.

A nice thing about being a doctor is that you have discretionary income. Lots of good people around here pay their bills in cash. One never knows what's in a doctor's pocket.

After passing the story around that Jackson had put his own screwdriver through his own eye, killing himself, we passed the story around that surprisingly enough Jackson had left a decent amount of insurance money. People believed us. They had to. Elizabeth was one of the original sources of the story, and who wouldn't believe Elizabeth? Anna put plumbing and electricity in that house, had it painted and repaired inside and out. Where else would she have gotten the money? After a few years, we passed the story that a French Canadian uncle of Anna had died, leaving her an extra little bit of money.

Anna lived well, though not exactly as well as I wanted her to live.

By that feminine instinct of hers, Anna always seemed to know when I was coming. Some nights, when I was getting out of the car, her front door would open. Naked, Anna would stand poised in the open doorway, the moonlight gleaming on her wonderful skin. She sure knew how to greet a fellow. She never lost her figure. I guess to make up for all those years of flapping laundry and junk outside her house, Anna worked hard and made a beautiful, extensive garden. Some afternoons we'd just sit quietly in chairs she had set out in the garden, Anna and I, Patty playing around at our feet, and drink iced tea or lemonade.

I don't remember too many actual conversations with Anna. She knew little of the town gossip, of course, not being a church-goer, not having a job in town. We'd just sit there in the garden, silently, like a couple of spent tourists in the world, just enjoying the sunlight and shade, birds and flowers, Patty, and each other.

Anna's garden was beautiful, three seasons of the year, and her lemonade and tea were always good. Of course she couldn't bake worth a damn.

A few years after Jackson was taken from us, as they say down at the church, you'd never know from looking at his old place he'd ever existed.

In bed, Anna and I were kids again. Nothing had changed. We were older but together we always had the energies of kids first discovering each other. Our bodies were endlessly interesting to each other, endlessly curious, inventive, enthusiastic, energetic. We made love so much, whenever I could get there to her house, usually for as long as I could stay, it's a wonder, but no two times were ever the same.

Anna and I never did anything to prevent her getting pregnant, never even talked about it. We just flung ourselves at each other whenever we came together. I suppose the years of Jackson's maltreatment rendered Anna incapable of bearing more children. Her body always retained some of the blue marks. Too bad. I would not have minded having a few bastards around town. I mean, bastards of my own.

Of course, over the years I came to feel almost as if Patty were my own. Mostly, it would be at night when I visited the house, but I was also there many times during the day, in the front room by the fireplace Anna had had built, or in the garden. Anna devoted herself to that child, saw she did well in school. She dressed Patty beautifully. I became fond of that child. Never will I forget the sound of her little voice, speaking to me, beginning every sentence with, "Doc?" to be sure she had my attention.

I never knew if Anna's and my continuing affair was known in the town. I doubt it, but I never really cared. Anna lived in an out-of-the-way place. When we met by happenstance in town, we met by happenstance. Still, we had little to say to each other. I doubt if Elizabeth ever knew. My hours were erratic; I was out as much at night as I was in anyway. Again, I really didn't care. What could Elizabeth say, or feel? You cannot kick a healthy thirty-year-old man out of bed, permanently, and then regret whatever he finds to do with himself. If Elizabeth, or others, ever knew about Anna and me I never heard a word or saw a sign of it.

Wait a minute. Hold down now. Just stay still . . . ah! Got you. One less fly in the world. There's another one . . . got him! The old boy can't be too slow.

Miss Slade came out of the house. She did not stop to close the screen door tightly. She looked out into the street and then at the old man.

"Doc," she said. "Your daughter is dead."

"You know, nurse, I've killed two flies just sitting here the last three minutes."

"Merciful heavens, what can I do to make him understand? DOC," she said. "YOUR DAUGHTER IS DEAD. Oh, please, God, let him hear me."

"In the house? Flies get everywhere. You ought to keep that screen door closed. Keep the flies out. I'll take care of the ones out here. Afternoon's getting on."

"Where is Steve?"

Hand over his eyebrows the old man looked at the sun slanting through the trees.

"DOC. HOLLY IS DEAD."

"Well, then, close the windows. A window must be open some-where. Did you look in the basement? A window is probably open in the basement."

"Oh, dear God. Merciful heavens."

A car stopped in front of the picket fence. A man with a black bag got out. He hurried through the gate and up the walk.

"How is she?" he asked Miss Slade.

She drew her shoulders back. "We lost her, Doctor."

"You did everything you could. Let's have a look at her."

They went into the house.

That's the young doctor now. He comes nearly every day. He came yesterday, I think, and the day before. Or was it this morning? He comes quite a lot. New young doctor. Probably doesn't know much. I wonder if he passed his examinations honestly. He probably did. He probably can't cheat worth a damn. You have to be a good cheater in a small town where you don't have many other facilities. That young doc comes to the house so often I wonder if he's padding his bill. That's the wrong kind of cheatin'.

Steve came into the yard. He had seen the doctor's car. He hurried up the steps to the porch.

"Hello there, Steve," Doc said.

Steve went by him into the house.

"The doctor's inside," the old man said. "The new young doctor I brought into the world, goddamn it."

He's the doctor now. The one they send for, listen to, trust. What does old Doc John know? He just sits on his front porch, readin' and swattin' flies. Damn. That one got away. How'd he do that? Crafty fly. There! Got him, after all! There are still no flies on old Doc John. Got that one, too!

They all die but old Doc John.

The doctor came out. He stopped by the old man and put his hand on the skinny shoulder. He was a young man, with short hair and heavy-rimmed glasses.

"I'm sorry, old Doc. Holly has passed on."

"What? Oh, yes, that's right. Say, why don't you give her a laxative now, a good cleaning-out, and stop all this traipsing back and forth? You're trying to make payments on that fancy car?"

The doctor squeezed the old man's shoulder and went down to his car and got in.

Doc John watched him. He hoped the young man did not object to his humorous remark about the car. There had to be humor among the medical fraternity. Everything was too serious not to laugh. He watched the car start up and make a U-turn in the street and go on to some other house.

Steve came out of the house.

Miss Slade followed him. She was looking worriedly at the boy.

Steve had his hands stuck in the back pockets of his jeans and his head was down.

Doc John noticed that neither of them took care to close the screen door tightly.

"Jesus Christ," said Steve. "Jesus Christ, Jesus Christ, Jesus Christ."

"Steve, I'm sorry," Miss Slade said. "We did everything possible for her. It's the Lord's will."

"Well, Jesuschrist that lord."

"Take it easy, son."

"Don't you 'son' me. You old bitch."

"Are there still some flies in the house?" the old man asked Miss Slade. "I've killed quite a few of them."

"No, no, Doc." Miss Slade put her hand on Steve's arm. "Cry, Steve. That's the thing to do."

"What's there to cry about? She lived her stinking little life in a stinking little town. And now she's dead. One less voice in the stinking church choir. That's all her death means to this town. Well, that's not going to happen to me. I'm getting out."

"Steve, you can't go. There's your grandfather."

"Golly," Doc John said. "There's another fly. Hold on, now. Ah! Got him!"

"Let the stinking church bury my mother. Let the stinking town take care of that old man. I don't care. I've got to get out of here!"

"Steve!" Miss Slade tried to shake the boy's arm. "It's okay to cry!"

"I won't cry! And I won't bury my mother! OLD MAN, YOU'RE JUST A PILE OF GARBAGE! YOU'RE THE ONE WHO SHOULD BE DEAD! NOT MY MOTHER!"

"That's right. Yes, indeed, Steve, that's exactly right. Sometimes I think bugs are just born to be killed. Don't see any other use for them; never have. They don't live long anyway, or contribute a damned thing, as far as I've been able to make out. They just buzz around and buzz around and then sit down and wait to get swatted. Look at all these dead flies. There: another one! See? There's no meaning to 'em at all."

"STOP SAYING THAT, GODDAMN IT!"

"Please, Steve. Just cry it out. You're just hurting yourself. You're saying things you don't mean, can't mean—"

"You go to hell."

Steve went into the house, slamming the screen door.

Miss Slade said, "Oh, Doc. Tell him he has to stay. He has to arrange his mother's funeral. He'll never forgive himself. He has to take care of you."

"Do you have a fly swatter in the house? Ask Holly if she knows where a fly swatter is."

"Merciful heavens." Miss Slade put both her hands to her face. "Merciful heavens."

Doc John said, "Bugs got you?"

Steve came out. He folded his wallet and slipped it into his back pocket.

"Steve," Miss Slade said. "I have to leave right away. I've been ordered on another case."

"I don't care."

"Steve, you can't do this!"

"Nurse Jane, I don't give one goddamn what this town thinks of me. I won't be here to know about it."

"Your grandfather, Steve!"

"He can rot."

Steve went down the steps.

"Bye, Steve," the old man called after him. "Play good."

6

I must have fallen asleep for a moment. More than a moment. Sun's gone behind that house over there. I wonder what time it is.

"Holly?

"Miss Slade?"

Steve should be getting home for supper pretty soon.

I wonder if Holly will be up for supper. No reason why she shouldn't be. The *virus,* as they now package it, doesn't take that long. She sure has had plenty of attention from that young doctor. Must remember to tease her about it. She ought to be getting up now. Too much time in bed does more harm than good. Stiffens the back. Turns everything to fat.

I expect we'll be saying good bye to Steve pretty soon. Every young fellow wants to go to the city, until he gets there. Until he sees the pigeons. Then, usually, he wants to come home again. If he's got any sense. By the time you're Steve's age, you sort of run out of small town, or think you do. Plenty of things happen in a small town over a lifetime to keep you interested. In a small town, things have a way of unhiding themselves. After life in a small town you may not know everything about everybody, but you sure know a lot about yourself. Every young person should try the city, once in his lifetime. I expect some find they like it. The rest come home, wiser. Ready to watch the town change. Able to take that slow kind of change in himself, and other people.

There are plenty of surprises in a small town. Oh, yes. Plenty of surprises.

People you know all your life can surprise the hell out of you.

I thought I knew Anna pretty well. I thought I understood what there was between us. I thought she understood.

Big surprise.

Doc John's practical nurse-receptionist put an envelope on his desk one morning between his seeing patients. His name and office address were block-printed on the envelope, and it was marked *Personal.* Only mildly curious, he slit it open with his thumb.

Dear John:

I don't know how else to do this. You have been very good to Patty and me all these years, giving us plenty of money to live on, and all. Maybe you think I've been spending all the money you've given me, but I haven't. I've saved a lot of it. So it is with thanks that I tell you that by the time you receive this letter, Patty and I will have left town. We are going somewhere in the South to live. John, please do not try to find us. Patty is quite the young lady, now, and she deserves better than this town where she will always be the daughter of Jackson and the granddaughter of the town's unwed washerwoman. Mrs Anna Jackson and her daughter, Patricia, are going to find a new place to start.

This may be rough on you, my just leaving this way, without a word, personally, but I have never been sure you would just let me go. You have had me all these years. I mean, you know what happened between Jackson and me that night long ago, you know what I did, and I've always known, John, that if I wasn't agreeable to your wishes, or if I ever said I wanted something else or better, or to go away, start life over somewhere else with my daughter, you could turn me in, say I confessed to you what really happened that night, or something. I mean, you've really had me.

Therefore, I think it's better this way.

—A.

Doc John put the letter in his desk drawer and went into the reception room to greet the next patient.

What a Dear John letter. I doubt there has ever been another like it. After all those years, almost a lifetime, together as youngsters, together again as adults, loving each other passionately, or at least so I thought. How is it possible she did not know I loved her, really loved her? I know I said so enough times. I must have acted it, showed it, because I did love Anna. And the child.

And all those years she thought I was *using* her? To use her expression, that I *really had* her? That if she didn't go along with what I wanted I could and would make trouble for her?

How is it possible she thought such a thing?

The very thought, the shocking, dripping hot realization she had thought so, all those years, finally said so in her letter, made me feel like an awful cheater.

I had been thinking, feeling, *knowing* one thing, and she had been thinking, feeling, *knowing* quite another.

Apparently, there had been much passion between us, but not much sensitivity. It is true we never talked much. Never felt we had to.

It is awfully hard to know the truth of people.

Of course I never looked for Anna, or the child. I loved them too much for that. If they wanted to be gone, let them be gone. If I had found them, Anna just might feel threatened. I had never the slightest idea she considered me a threat. At decreasing intervals I haunted that house out there by Teatle's Crossroads Store. I watched the gardens go to weed. I had the hope Anna's was a temporary insanity, that one day or night I would go to the house, the door would open, Anna would be framed naked in the doorway, her skin catching whatever light. . . .

I never did anything about the little house Anna worked so hard to make pretty. Neither did she, I guess. She never sold it. Abandoned and vandalized, within a few years it looked again as if Jackson lived there.

No, I never got to say good bye to Anna properly, nor her child, Patty. How I wondered about them. My heart yearned for them. Their absence was a constant ache, for years.

But I would never pursue anyone, if it would give her pain.

Growing so old, the pain of missing people has to be worse than the pain of any death.

How often do I wish Elizabeth were still alive? Just every time I think of her, that's how often.

I wonder what Elizabeth would be like today. She'd be pretty old, of course. Probably cantankerous. Old people are apt to get cantankerous. She'd be as old as I am. Good gosh. That is old. I don't think I'd enjoy seeing Elizabeth that old. I suppose if Elizabeth were alive we'd sit out here on the porch shoutin' at each other like a couple of old loons.

It's been fifteen years now. That's been a long time without Elizabeth. She was companionable. I enjoyed her company, talking with her, listening to her, trading with her the news of the town, the little things. I was without her a long time before we were married and a long time without her since she passed away.

For just a short while in the middle of my life, I had Elizabeth.

Doc John had a call at his office from Holly. It was a Saturday in November.

"What's the matter, Holly?"

"Mom is sick, Dad. Very sick. You'd better come home."

Elizabeth was in bed. She looked frightened.

Unwillingly, she let him examine her. He found advanced cancer of the stomach. He did not need tests to see that now. He had seen enough of it.

At first he blamed himself for not having noticed it. But she was seventy and they had not had carnal knowledge of each other in forty years. They had not slept in the same bed. Deliberately she had concealed her illness with corsets and makeup. His hours were so irregular he had given up noticing her eating habits long before. She could always say she had eaten. If he had noticed her illness there was not much he could have done about it.

It took her three weeks to die. During those three weeks she lay in her bed sweating a little and looking frightened. With his pills and needles he made sure she had as little pain as possible. Doc John had to go out on other calls. When he returned to the house he would sit on the edge of her bed with his head in his hands. She knew she was dying. She had known it before he did. A doctor's wife has a terrible knowledge. She had concealed her illness to spare him.

After three weeks Elizabeth's head rolled over on the pillow and the frightened feeling in the room was gone.

Doc John handled her as he would any other dead body. He had been trained to do that.

The strange thing, and John knew at the time it was strange, was that after Elizabeth died and John had called the undertaker and told him to come to the house, he got into his Winslow car and drove around, first to the big old house on the hill in the woods where Amy played out her life on the piano, even down the wood lane, stopping a moment, to confirm the silence, then past Tatie Hill where those two tall pine trees still stood, between which John had first made love, slowly, slowly past Elizabeth's family home, seeing the copper beech tree still there on the lawn, trying to see into the deep, empty, shady porch as he drove by, slowly by the house where Anna lived, abandoned now. It was not just to Elizabeth that John was saying good bye at seventy, it was to some vast part of himself, his youth, his vitality, to most of life, the good and the bad, and he knew that.

It's getting late. Colder, too. I wonder where Steve is. He should be coming home about now. In a while they'll drag the old man in for the night. Take him away from the night ozone. They never have left me out this late. It's almost dark. I'll stay until they call me. They'll call me soon.

Yep, being sad too long makes you unworthy of life. You have to see life as a whole, the peaks and the valleys all together. 'Course, I guess you're pretty old before you get to see life that way. When you're young you're either in a peak or in a valley. Smooth, smooth is what you are when you're old.

If there is a God, forgive me, but I'll never understand why babies die. Not if I live to be a hundred.

And here I am, an old man, and I get to live it all over in my thoughts.

Maybe I will tell Steve about Olson's kids when he gets back for supper. He'll like that story. He can stand an illusion. Too, the young always like to hear about each other.

I wonder what Holly has fixed for supper. Probably something from packages. They all use packages these days. Holly's sick. That's right. Holly's sick. Well, she'll get better. She's young yet. She just needed a rest. Been workin' too hard, down at the bank. She might be up for supper.

Steve should get a kick out of that story about Olson's daughter. He might not believe it. Such innocence is hard to believe.

Say, it is getting colder. The sun must be all the way down. Even the sunset is over.

"Holly? Holly?"

Is the door closed? She probably can't hear me. I've thought lately Holly is getting a little hard of hearing.

"Miss Slade?"

The old man saw Steve come up the steps in the dark. His legs were long and his head was low.

"Hello there, Steve."

"Hello."

The boy took out his package of cigarettes and gave one to the old man, and lit it for him.

"Thank you very kindly, sir," *the old man said.*

The boy stood over the old man, smoking.

This was the boy's gesture toward the old man the old man liked best. He had always felt most intimate with his grandson, smoking with him this way.

"Steve, did I ever tell you that story about Olson and his starving daughter?"

"No, sir, you never did."

"That's a good story. You'd like to hear it."

"I don't believe you ever told it to me, sir."

"Well, I ought to. It's a good one. It's about young people."

"Come on, Granddad. You must be cold. Come on in the house for some supper."

"Supper? Oh, okay. I thought it was late. I was just thinking of going in myself. I'll tell you that story of Olson's daughter later. It's a wonderful story, son."